THE SOMME

VOLUME I

THE FIRST BATTLE OF THE SOMME
(1916–1917)

(ALBERT — BAPAUME — PÉRONNE)

THE FRANCO - BRITISH OFFENSIVE OF THE SOMME (1916).

THE OBJECTIVES OF THE OFFENSIVE.

In June, 1916, the enemy were the attacking party ; the Germans were pressing Verdun hard, and the Austrians had begun a vigorous offensive against the Italians. It therefore became necessary for the Allies to make a powerful effort to regain the initiative of the military operations.

The objectives of the Franco-British offensive were, to regain the initiative of the military operations ; to relieve Verdun ; to immobilise the largest possible number of German divisions on the western front, and prevent their transfer to other sectors ; to wear down the fighting strength of the numerous enemy divisions which would be brought up to the front of attack.

GENERAL FOCH, IN COMMAND OF THE FAYOLLE - MICHELER ARMY GROUP, DURING THE SOMME OFFENSIVE OF 1916.

Thanks to the immense effort made by the entire British Empire, their army had considerably increased in men and material, and was now in a position to undertake a powerful offensive.

Under the command of Field-Marshal Haig, two armies, the 4th (General Rawlinson) and the 2nd (General Gough) were to take part in the offensive.

In spite of the terrible strain France was undergoing at Verdun, the number of troops left before that fortress, under the command of General Pétain, who had thoroughly consolidated the defences, was reduced to the strictest minimum, and the 6th and 10th Armies, under the command of General Fayolle and General Micheler, respectively, were thus able to collaborate with the British in the Somme offensive.

Within a few days of the enemy's formidable onslaught of June 23 against the Thiaumont—Vaux front, in which seventeen German regiments took part (see the Michelin Guide : " VERDUN, AND THE BATTLES FOR ITS POSSESSION "), the Allied offensive was launched (July 1).

The Theory, Methods and Tactics adopted

With both sides entrenched along a continuous front, the predominating problem was : How to break through the enemy's defences to the open ground beyond the last trenches, and then force the final decision.

In 1915, the Allies had endeavoured unsuccessfully to solve it ; in 1916, the Germans, in turn, had suffered their severest check before Verdun.

Putting experience to profit, the Allies now sought to apply the methods of piercing on broader lines.

The defences having increased in strength and depth, the blow would require to be more powerful, precise, and concentrated as to space and time.

After the attacks of September, 1915, the French Staff set down as an axiom that " material cannot be combatted with men." Consequently, no more attacks without thorough preparation ; nothing was to be left to chance.

The orders issued to the different arms, divisions, battalions, batteries, air-squadrons, etc., were recorded in voluminous plans of attack, the least of which numbered a hundred pages.

Thousands of aerial photographs were taken and assembled ; countless maps, plans and sketches made. Everything connected with the coming drama was methodically arranged : the staging, distribution of the parts, the various acts.

Such was the intellectual preparation which, lasting several months, was carried out simultaneously with the equipping of the front line.

Equipping the Front Line

Preparing for a modern battle is a Herculean task. At a sufficient distance behind the front line immense ammunition and revictualling depôts are established. Miles of railway, both narrow and normal gauge, have to be put down, to bring up supplies to the trenches. Existing roads have to be improved, and new ones made. In the Somme, long embankments had to be built across the marshy valleys, as well as innumerable shelters for the combatants, dressing-stations, and sheds for storing the ammunition, food, water, engineering supplies, etc. Miles of deep communicating trenches, trenches for the telephone wires, assembly trenches, parallels and observation-posts had to be made. The local quarries were worked, and wells bored.

4

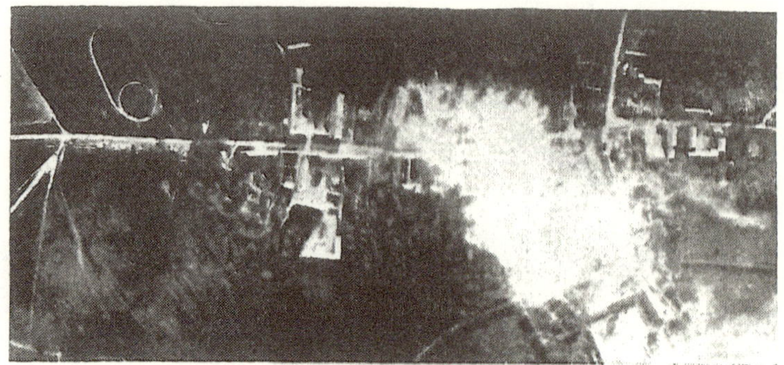

Ginchy, bombarded by the British on July 11, 1916.

Ginchy, ten days later (July 21, 1916).

Ginchy, two days before capture by the British (Sept. 7, 1916). See p. 86.

ILLUSTRATING THE PROGRESSIVE DESTRUCTION AND LEVELLING OF A VILLAGE BY ARTILLERY.

FIRING A 12-INCH LONG-RANGE GUN.

The Part Played by each Arm in the Different Phases of the Attack

In modern, well-ordered battle, it is the material strength which counts most. The cannon must crush the enemy's machine-guns. Superiority of artillery is an essential element of success.

According to the latest formula, "the artillery conquers, the infantry occupies."

At each stage of the battle, each arm has a definite role to play.

The Artillery

Before the battle, the artillery must destroy the enemy's wire entanglements, trenches, shelters, blockhouses, observation-posts, etc.; locate and engage his guns; hamper and disperse his working parties.

During the battle, it must crush enemy resistance, provide the attacking infantry with a protecting screen of fire, by means of creeping barrages, and cut off the defenders from supplies and reinforcements by isolating barrages.

After the battle, it must protect the attacking troops who have reached their objectives, from enemy counter-attacks, by barrage fire.

CAMOU-FLAGED HEAVY GUN ABOUT TO FIRE.

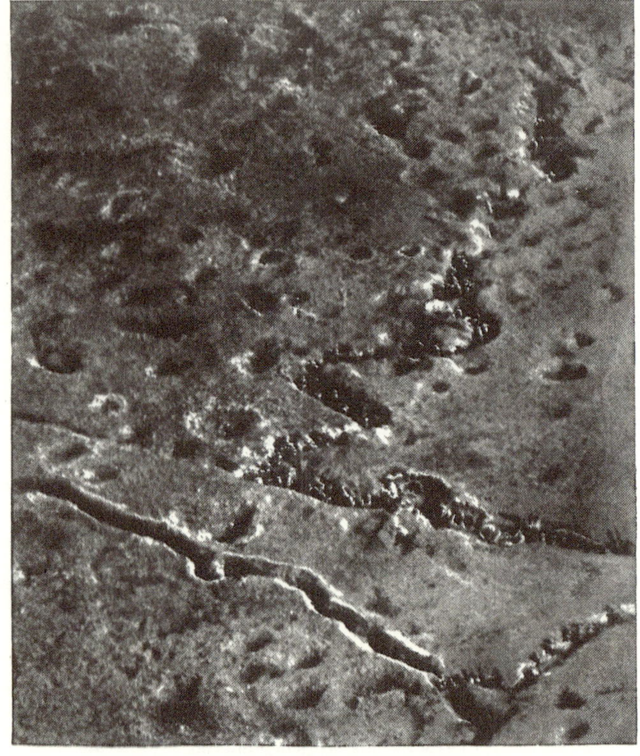

THE CAPTURE OF VERMANDOVILLERS.

The arrival of French reinforcements.   Photographed from accompanying aeroplane at 600 feet 'p. 128).

The Infantry

Before the battle, the attacking troops assemble first in the shelters, then in the assembling places and parallels made during the previous night.   The battalion, company and section commanders survey the ground of attack with field-glasses.

During the battle, at a given signal, the assaulting battalions dash forward from the departure trenches, the first wave deployed in skirmishing order ; the second and third, consisting of trench-cleaners, machine-gunners and supports, follow thirty or forty yards behind, in short columns (single file or two abreast).   Reinforcements *echeloned,* and likewise in small columns, bring up the rear, 150 to 200 yards behind.

As a matter of fact, in actual fighting, each regiment attacks separately. The Commandant, realising the difficulties on the spot, must have in hand all the necessary means of success, the most powerful being the artillery, which accompanies and prepares each phase and development of the attack.

INFANTRY ADVANCE.

The attacking waves mark their advance with Bengal lights.

Generally, the creeping barrage, timed beforehand, is loosed at the same moment of time as the assaulting wave. The infantry follows as closely as possible.

Constant and perfect *liaison* is necessary between the infantry and artillery. This is ensured by means of runners, pennons, panels, telephones, optical telegraphy, signals, rockets, Bengal lights, etc. A similar *liaison* is ensured between the various attacking units, on the right, left and behind. Action must be co-ordinated, an essential point on which the G.H.Q. always strongly insist.

As soon as the enemy perceives the assaulting waves, every effort is made to scatter them by means of artillery barrage and machine-gun fire, asphyxiating gas, grenades and liquid fire, so that generally the storming troops cross " no man's land " through a veritable screen of fire. The enemy's fire likewise extends to the first-line trenches, to cut off the first waves from their supports.

Without stopping at the enemy's first-line organisations, the first attacking wave overwhelms the position, annihilates all defenders encountered, and only comes to a halt at the assigned objective. The following waves support the first one, and deal with points of resistance. The trench-cleaners or moppers-up " clean out " the position of enemy survivors with bayonet, knife and grenade, in indescribable death grapples. Progress is slow along the communicating trenches, and in the underground shelters, tunnels, cellars and ruins, where the defenders have taken refuge. From time to time hidden machine-guns are unmasked and have to be captured.

After the attack.—As soon as the " cleaning out " is finished, any prisoners

GERMAN PRISONERS HURRYING TO
THE ALLIES' LINES.

are sent to the rear, being often forced to cross their own barrage-fire. Meanwhile the other defenders will have withdrawn to their positions of support.

Having reached their objective, the assaulting troops must hold their ground. Sentries are posted, while the rest of the men consolidate the position in view of the inevitable counter-attack, which is generally not long in coming.

Under bombardment, the levelled trenches have to be re-made, the shell-holes organised and flanked with machine-guns, and communications with the rear ensured for the bringing up of stores and, if necessary, reinforcements.

The assaulting troops may thus reach their objectives without excessive losses or nervous strain, and may be kept in line for a second and third similar effort, after a few days' rest, during which the artillery will have destroyed the next enemy positions.

The Flying Corps

Before the battle.—Metaphorically speaking, the Flying Corps (aeroplanes and observation balloons) is the " eye " of the High Command, which largely depends on it for precise information regarding the enemy's movements and positions. It likewise regulates the artillery fire, and furnishes that arm with photographs, showing exactly the progress made by the destruction

OBSERVATION BALLOON.

bombardments. Another equally important duty is to " blind the enemy " by destroying their aeroplanes and observation balloons.

During the battle.—Flying low, sometimes within a few hundred feet of the ground, the airmen furnish invaluable information, and often photographs, showing the progress of the attack, the *terrain* being marked out with panels and Bengal lights. They also often attack the enemy with their machine-guns.

BRITISH TANKS MAKE THEIR DÉBUT.

After the battle.—The massing of enemy troops for counter-attacks is signalled to the artillery, which regulates its barrages accordingly, then, working in *liaison*, the two services "prepare" the ground for the next attack.

These tactics were gradually perfected on the Somme battlefields, where the Germans learned by costly experience to improve their defences.

The offensive methods acquired also greater suppleness, and the new arm—**the tank**—came to the relief of the infantry.

GENERAL FAYOLLE INSPECTING THE CONQUERED LINES.

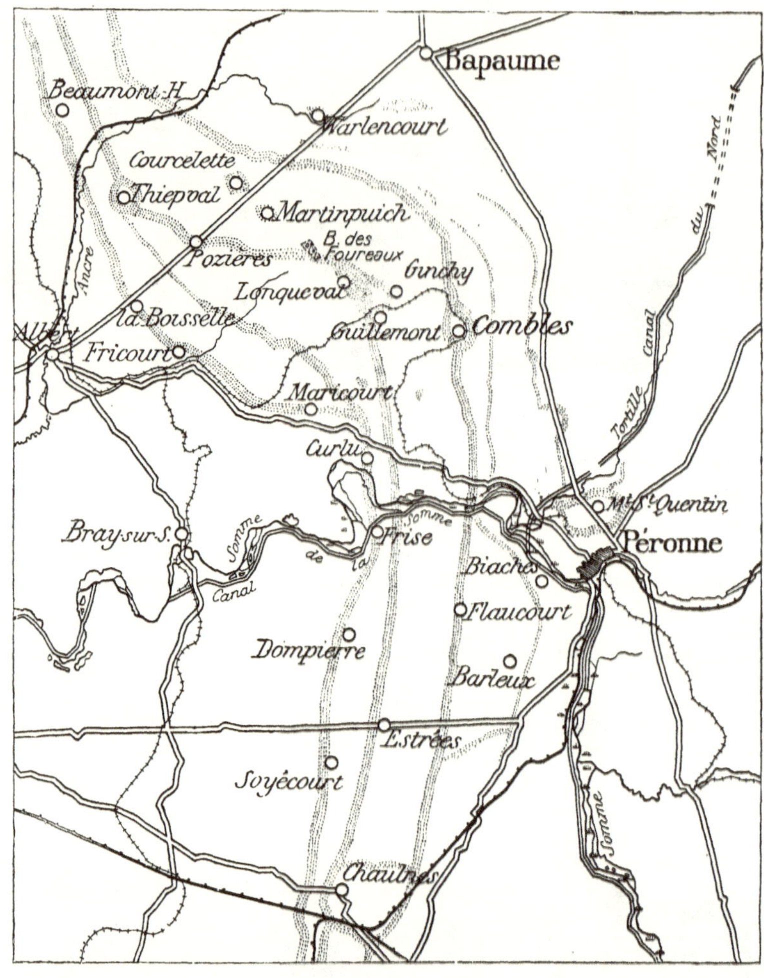

THE DOTTED ZONES REPRESENT THE GERMAN LINES OF RESISTANCE.

THE SOMME BATTLEFIELD.

The battle extended over the Picardy plateau, south and north of the Somme. Before the war, the region was rich and fertile, the chalky ground having a covering of alluvial soil of variable thickness.

The slopes of the undulating hills and the broad table-lands were covered with immense fields of corn, poppies and sugar beet. Here and there were small woods—vestiges of the Arrouaise Forest, which covered the whole country in the Middle-Ages. There were scarcely any isolated houses, but occasionally a windmill, farm or sugar-refinery would break the monotony of the landscape.

The villages were surrounded with orchards, and their low, red-tiled houses were generally grouped around the church. The plateau was crossed by wide, straight roads bordered with fine elms.

The war has robbed the district of its former aspect. The ground, in a state of complete upheaval, is almost levelled in places, while the huge mine-craters give it the appearance of a lunar landscape. The ground was churned up so deeply that the upper covering of soil has almost entirely disappeared and the limestone substratum now laid bare is overrun with rank vegetation. From Thiepval to Albert, Combles and Péronne, and from Chaulnes to Roye, the ground was so completely upturned as to render it useless for agriculture for many years to come, and a scheme to plant this area with pine trees is now being considered.

Nearly all the villages were razed, and now form so many vast heaps of débris. This battlefield is a striking example of the total destructions wrought by the late war.

The Topography of the Ground and the Enemy Defence-works

North of the Somme.—The battle zone, bounded by the rivers Ancre, Somme and Tortille—the latter doubled by the Northern Canal—forms a strongly undulating plateau (altitude 400–520 feet), which descends in a series of hillocks, separated by deep depressions, to the valleys of the rivers (altitude 160 feet). The Albert—Combles—Péronne railway runs along the bottom of one of these depressions.

The higher parts of the plateau form a ridge, one of whose tapering extremities rests on the Thiepval Heights, on the bank of the Ancre. Running west to east, the ridge crosses the Albert-Bapaume road at Pozières, passes Foureaux Wood, then north of Ginchy. It is the watershed which divides the rivers flowing northwards to the Escaut and southwards to the Somme.

The second line of German positions was established on this ridge, while the first line extended along the undulating slopes which descended towards the Allies' positions. There were other enemy positions on the counter-slopes behind the ridge.

These positions took in the villages and small woods of the region, all of which, fortified during the previous two years, bristled with defence-works and machine-guns.

Some of these villages (Courcelette, Martinpuich, Longueval, Guillemont and Combles), hidden away in hollows, were particularly deadly for the Allies ; the defenders, unseen, were able to snipe the assailants as they appeared on the hill tops. The Allies had to encircle these centres of resistance before they were able to enter them.

South of the Somme.—The battle zone, bounded by the large circular bend of the Somme at Péronne, formed a kind of arena. The vast, flat table-lands of the Santerre district, separated by small valleys, descend gently towards the large marshy valley of the Somme, in which the canal runs parallel with the river.

Owing to the narrowness of this zone, the Germans were forced to establish their positions close behind one another, and the latter were therefore in danger of being carried in a single rush. On the other hand, the assailants, rapid advance was first hampered, then held by the marshy valley, which prevented them from following up their brilliant initial success.

During the battle, the Germans, driven from their first positions, hastily prepared new ones, and clung desperately to the counter-slopes of the hills which descend to the valleys.

The Different Stages of the Offensive

The offensive of the Somme, the general direction of which was towards Cambrai, aimed at reaching the main northern line of communications, by opening a gap between Bapaume and Péronne.

The main sector of attack—between the Ancre and the Somme—was flanked on either side by diversion sectors north of the Ancre and south of the Somme.

Putting to profit the German failure at Verdun, where the enemy masses, after appalling sacrifice of human life, gradually became blocked in a narrow sector (7½ miles in width), the Allies widened their front of attack.

After an effective " pounding " by the guns which annihilated all obstacles to a considerable depth, the assaulting waves went forward simultaneously along a 24-mile front, feeling for a weak sector where a breach could be made. The attack was a complete success in the diversion sector, south of the Somme, thanks to the nature of the ground, but, as previously stated, it was not possible to follow it up immediately.

North of the Somme the British offensive was held.

Warned by the immense preparations, the Germans were not taken unawares. Their reserves flowed in and resisted on new defensive positions. The advance of the French 6th Army was slowed down to correspond with that of the British.

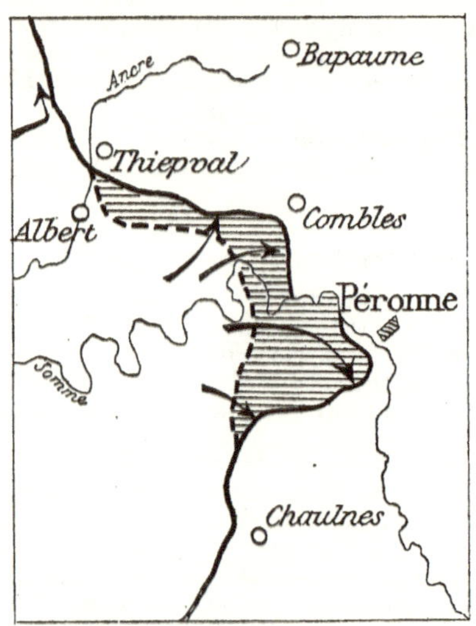

ATTEMPTED BREAK-THROUGH.

A breach was made south of the Somme, but the marshes prevented development, while to the north, the offensive was held on the Ancre lines.

The Battle of Attrition

(See the sketch-maps on pages 13, 18, 27.)

This attempted break-through (July 1–12) soon changed into a battle of attrition (July 14, 1916, to March, 1917).

The Allies' plan now was gradually to shatter the German resistance by a continuous push along the whole line, and by vigorous action at the various strong-points.

The gains of ground diminished, but the German reserves were gradually used up. In spite of their hastily constructed system of new defences, the Germans realised the precarious nature of their new lines, and were forced, in March, 1917, to fall back and shorten their front.

THE PHASES OF THE BATTLE OF ATTRITION.

NORTH OF THE SOMME.   SOUTH OF THE SOMME.

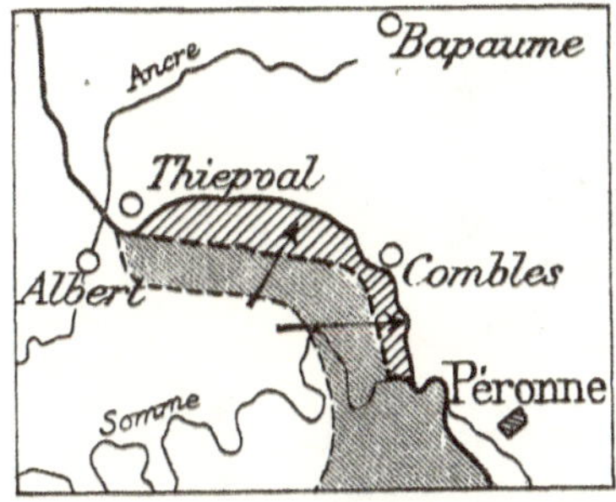

The Franco-British troops enlarge the conquered positions and attack the centres of resistance: Combles and Thiepval (July 14—September 1).

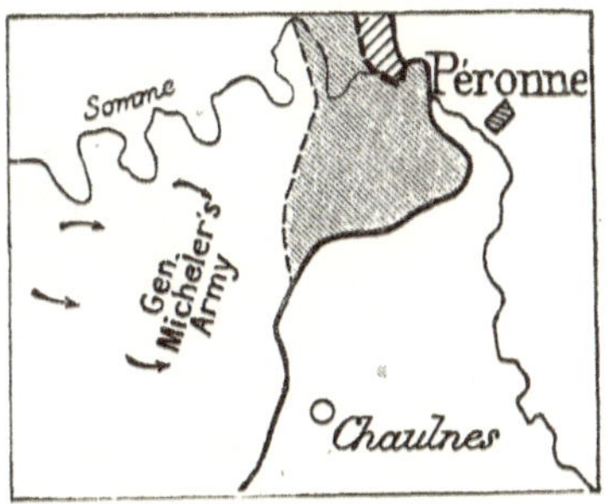

The 6th Army (French) held by the Somme Marshes, took up its new position. The 10th Army (French) assembled on its right (August—September).

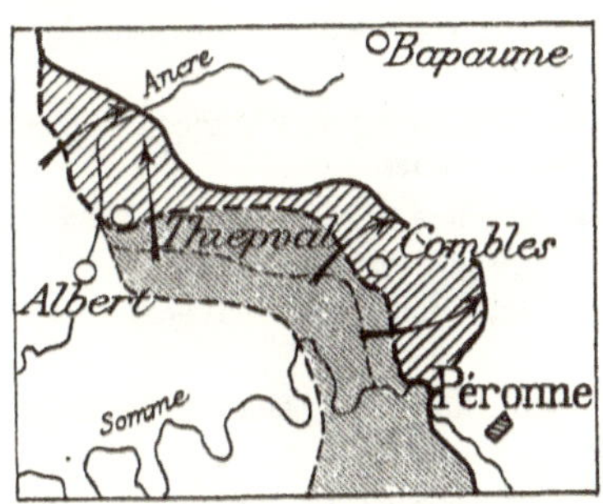

Combles and Thiepval turned and conquered, after being surrounded (September—November).

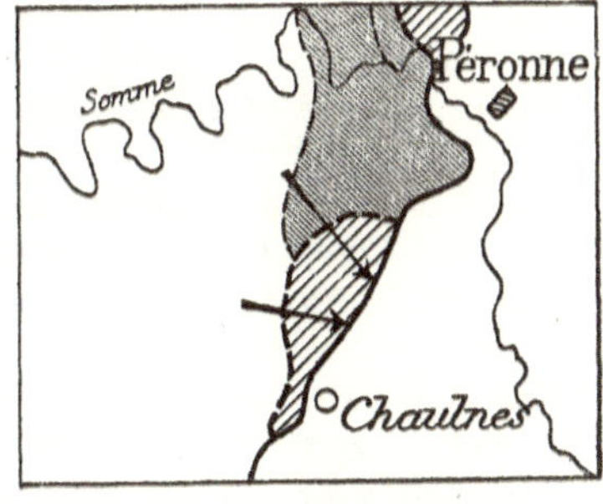

The 10th Army attacked, but was held in front of Chaulnes (September—October).

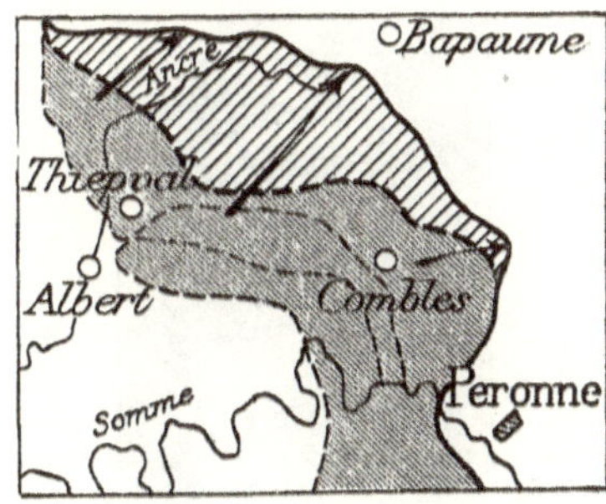

The Allies advance toward their main objectives: Bapaume and Péronne (November—March).

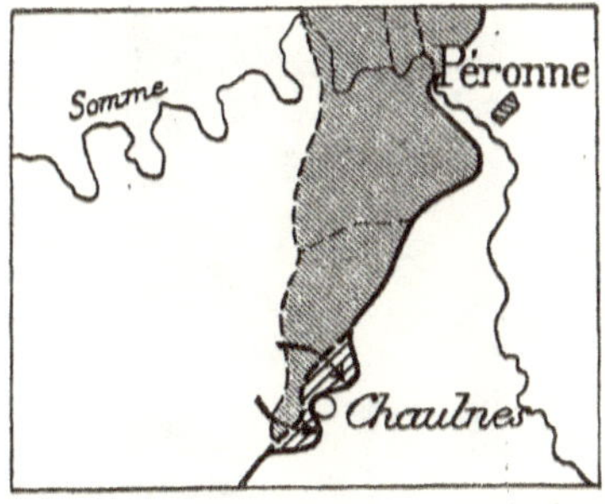

The 10th Army (French) failed to encircle Chaulnes, and consolidated its new positions (October—November).

FIELD-MARSHAL HAIG.

THE ATTEMPTED BREAK-THROUGH.

The British Attack

On July 1, the front of attack, about 21 miles long, extended from Gommécourt to Maricourt.

The attack was made by the 4th Army (Gen. Rawlinson), comprising five army corps, and by three divisions of the right wing of the 3rd Army (Gen. Allenby).

The main sector of attack, lying between the Ancre and Maricourt, forms a 90° salient, the summit of which encircled Fricourt.

The first German positions included Ovillers, La Boisselle, Fricourt, Mametz and Montauban, and formed the objective of the attack.

The latter, directed generally towards Bapaume, was delivered against both flanks of the salient.

From the start, the attack was held before the western side of the salient, in spite of the great heroism of the British.

The right wing, on the southern side, succeeded in carrying the first German position.

In face of this result, Field-Marshal Haig decided to push home the attack

Photo, Russell, London.

GENERAL RAWLINSON.

Photo, F. A. Swaine, London

GENERAL ALLENBY.

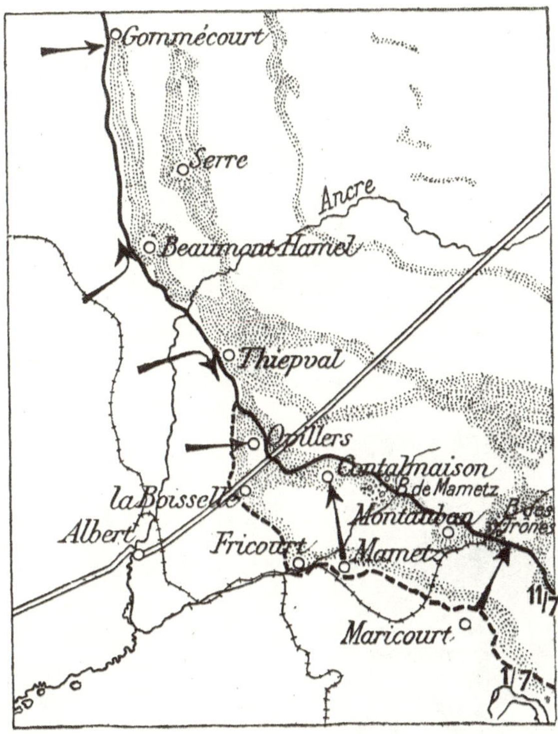

on his right (three corps under Gen. Rawlinson), while his left (two corps under Gen. Gough) would continue to press the enemy, and thus form the pivot of the manœuvre.

The first assaults on July 1 gave the British Montauban and Mametz, while Fricourt and La Boisselle were encircled and carried on July 3. Progress continued on the right, Contalmaison and Mametz Wood, reached on the 5th, were carried on the 11th.

On the extreme right, the British, in *liaison* with the French, reached the southern edges of Trônes Wood, and came into contact with the second German positions. Over 6,000 prisoners were taken. The Germans launched incessant counter-attacks without result.

In the diversion sector, north of the Ancre, the initial successes at Gommécourt, Serre and on the Ancre could not be followed up.

The Germans continued to hold Beaumont-Hamel and Thiepval in force.

Photo, "*Daily Mirror*" *Studios.*
GENERAL GOUGH.

The French Attack

The French 6th Army (Gen. Fayolle) attacked along a ten-mile front, astride of the Somme, from Maricourt to Soyécourt, in the general direction of Péronne.

North of the Somme.—The 20th Corps had to conquer the German first position, consisting of three or four lines of trenches connected by numerous *boyaux* to the fortified woods and village of Curlu.

This position was carried in a single rush on July 1, and consolidated on the three following days.

The second and third German positions were as strong as the first, and included the villages of Hardecourt and Hem. On the 5th, Hem and the plateau which dominates the village to the north were taken. On the 8th, the French, in *liaison* with the British, first carried, then progressed beyond, Hardecourt.

From July 1 to 8, the 20th Corps captured the first and second German positions and consolidated their conquest on the following days.

GENERAL FAYOLLE.

South of the Somme.—The attack was launched on July 1, two hours later than that on the northern bank. With fine dash, the 1st Colonial Corps and a division of Brittany reserves carried the first German position, including the villages of Dompierre, Becquincourt and Fay.

On the 2nd, the movement was continued on the left. Frise, outflanked from the south, was captured, Méréaucourt Wood encircled, and Herbécourt carried by a frontal attack, after being turned from the north. The approaches to Assevillers and Estrées were reached. The northern part of the second position was captured.

On the 3rd, the advance continued on the left. Flaucourt, in the third position, was carried in the course of an extraordinarily daring *coup-de-main*. Assevillers likewise fell.

Belloy was captured on the 4th; the divisional cavalry patrolled freely as far as the Somme, between Biaches and Barleux.

Biaches village and La Maisonnette observation-post fell on the 9th and 10th. The horses of the African Mounted Chasseurs were watered in the Somme, and the Zouaves gathered cherries in the suburban gardens of Péronne.

During these ten days the French troops, by carrying out a vast turning movement on the left, towards the south-east, had pierced all the German positions. A breach had been made, but the marshy valley of the Somme in this diversion sector made it very difficult to follow up the success; moreover, the objectives assigned to these troops did not provide for such exploitation.

The French attack had been carried out with great dash. In addition to

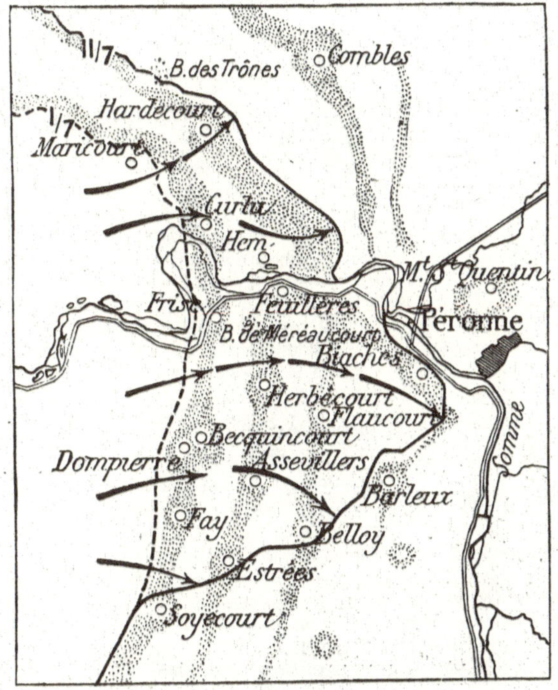

the many lines of defences, villages and fortified woods conquered, 85 guns, 100 machine-guns, and 26 minenwerfer were captured, and over 12,000 prisoners, including 235 officers, taken.

The gallant troops, which had thus inflicted a stinging defeat on the enemy, included the famous 20th Corps, which, a few months before, in a veritable inferno, had barred the road to Verdun.

THE SITE OF MONACU FARM ON THE MAUREPAS ROAD NEAR HEM WOOD.

THE BATTLE OF ATTRITION (North of the Somme).

In the main sector of attack the German line had not been completely broken. This attempt to break through was succeeded by a battle of attrition, in the course of which the Allies, working in close collaboration, dealt the enemy repeated blows.

North of the Somme.—After July 11, the Allied front between the Ancre and the Somme, held by the strong German positions of the Thiepval Plateau, passed in front of Contalmaison and Montauban. On the southern edges of Trônes Wood it turned southwards towards Hem.

This line formed a salient to the east of Trônes Wood—a narrow space bristling with guns. From the high ground of their second position in the north, and that of Longueval, Ginchy and Guillemont, the German firing line formed a semi-circle round this salient, which was threatened by incessant counter-attacks. While maintaining the pressure on the west, it became necessary for the Allies to widen the angle and enlarge the front, or, in other words, to obtain greater freedom of movement.

This was the aim of the various Franco-British thrusts during the second fortnight of July and in August.

1.—Widening the Front
(July 14—September 1.)

In order to support the forthcoming French thrust towards the east, a British attack to the north-east was deemed necessary.

The German second positions from Contalmaison to Trônes Wood, and the crests of the ridge of the plateau formed the objective.

On July 14, the 4th British Army, by a clever manœuvre, took up positions in the dark at attacking distance. Trônes Wood was carried on the first day. Longueval, stormed from east and west, was partly captured. In the centre, Bazentin-le-Grand with its wood and Bazentin-le-Petit were taken. To the left, the southern outskirts of Pozières were reached.

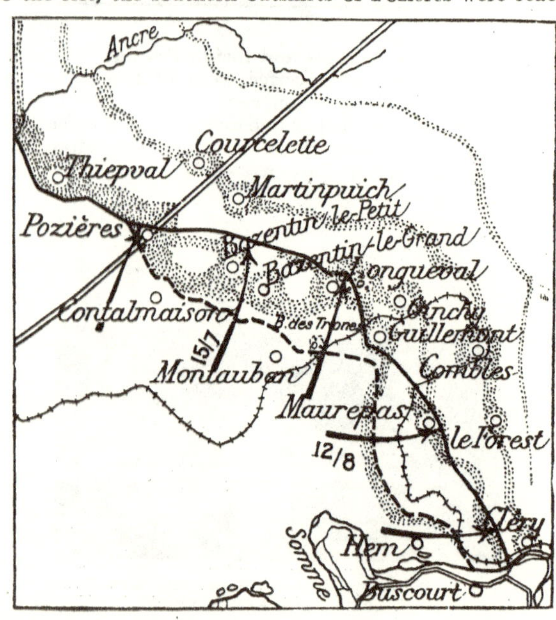

BRITISH GRAVES IN TRÔNES WOOD (*p.* 85).

On July 15–16, the British progressed beyond the German second position—carried along a three-mile front—and established their advance-posts in the vicinity of the German third position.

By this time the Germans had recovered from their set-back of the 14th and offered an aggressive defence. Counter-attacking at the point of the salient in the Allied lines at Delville Wood, they succeeded in slipping through, but they were held in front of Longueval.

On the 20th and 23rd, the Allies delivered a general attack. The British 4th Army was now confronted by the enemy in force all along the line. However, the village of Pozières, one of the strong-points of Thiepval Plateau, to the west, was carried by the Australians on July 25. The French advanced their lines as far as the ravine, in which runs the light railway from Combles to Cléry.

Hidden in a hollow of the ground, Guillemont resisted the British assaults of July 30 and August 7.

On August 12, the French 1st Corps continued its thrust eastwards, turning Guillemont from the south. The Zouaves and 1st Cambrai Infantry Regiment entered Maurepas.

More to the south, the 170th Infantry captured the fortified crest lying 1 km. 500 west of Cléry.

The British hung on to the western outskirts of Guillemont.

DELVILLE WOOD NORTH OF LONGUEVAL (*p.* 60).

2.—The Surrounding and Capture of the Main Centres of Resistance

On September 1, the British lines, still hanging on to the southern slopes of the Thiepval Plateau, followed the crest of the ridge north of the villages of Thiepval, Bazentin-le-Petit and Longueval, in front of the outskirts of Delville Wood, were then deflected south-east and joined with the French lines in the ravine of the Combles railway. The French lines surrounded Maurepas, then followed the road from Maurepas to Cléry. Thiepval and Combles seemed impregnable.

Instead of making a frontal attack against these positions, the Allies first turned and then surrounded them by a succession of thrusts.

In addition to their successive lines of defence-works, which included a number of villages, the Germans had transformed the little town of Combles, lying entirely hidden from view at the bottom of an immense depression—into a redoubtable fortress. A large garrison was safely sheltered in vast quarries connected by tunnels with the concrete defence-works.

The Surrounding and Capture of Combles

In September, four Allied thrusts were necessary to encircle and capture Combles (*see p.* 80):

The Attack of September 3

Ginchy and Guillemont formed the British objective. On the 3rd, in spite of machine-gun fire from Ginchy, the Irish carried Guillemont, which had resisted for seven weeks. Progressing beyond the village they reached and captured Leuze Wood, 1 km. 500 west of Combles. On the 9th, they enlarged their gains by the conquest of Ginchy (*see p.* 4).

The German positions connecting Combles with Le Forest and Cléry formed the French objective.

This position—defended by four German divisions—was carried with magnificent dash on the 3rd, from near Combles to the Somme.

On the 5th, the French progressed beyond the position and reached the following line : Anderlu Wood, north-east of Le Forest, Marrières Wood, and the crest north-east of Cléry ; 2,500 prisoners were taken.

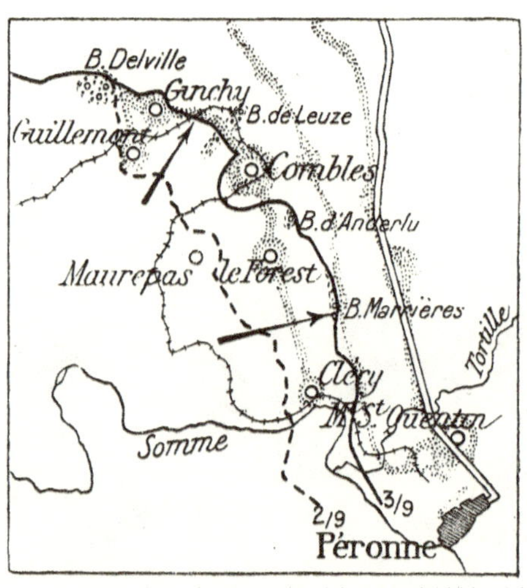

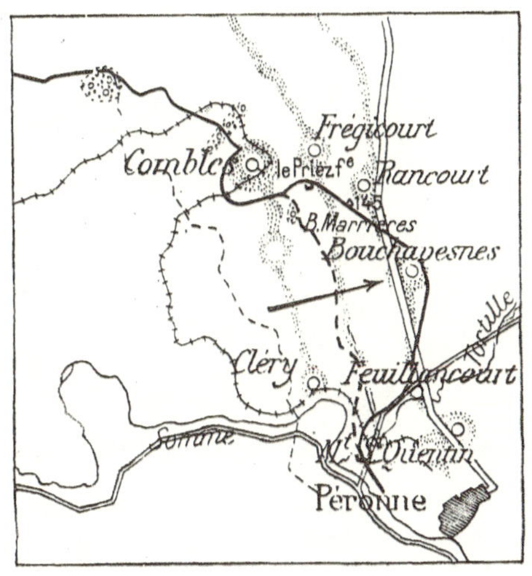

The French Attack of the 12th

Attacking again, the French were now confronted by two parallel lines of defences. The first position (known as the Berlingots' trenches) ran through Frégicourt, Le Priez Farm and Marrières Woods. The second position, along the National road, 2 km. behind the first, rested on Rancourt, Feuillancourt and the Canal du Nord, taking in Bouchavesnes.

Following close behind the creeping barrage, the attacking troops carried the Berlingots' trenches in half an hour. From there, the left wing attacked and captured Hill 145, and advanced as far as the National road, between Rancourt and Bouchavesnes. The right wing reached the Valley of the Tortille, opposite Feuillancourt.

Bouchavesnes, although not included in the objectives assigned to the storming troops, was next attacked, and at 8 p.m. Bengal lights, announcing its capture, were burning in the ruins of the village.

On the 13th, the French crossed the National road. The enemy showed great nervousness, and brought up three new divisions.

THE CANAL
DU NORD.

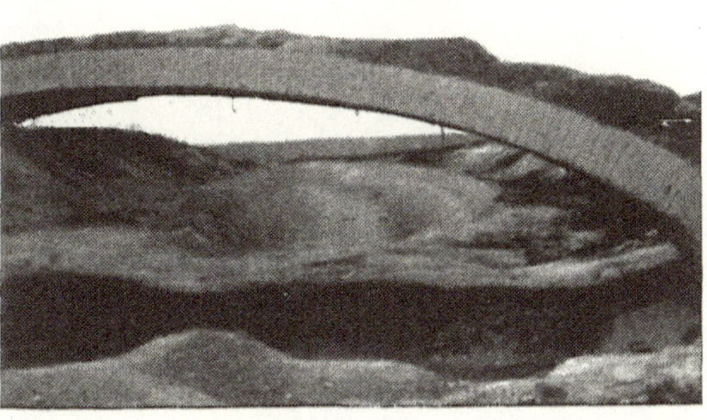

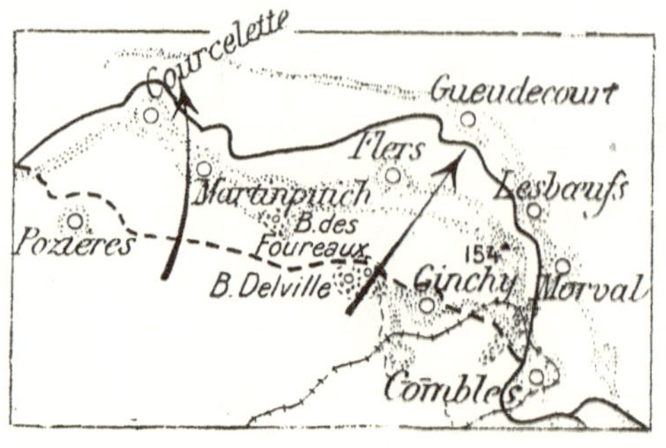

The British Attack of September 15

The German positions of Foureaux Wood, Hill 154 and Morval were the objectives of the attack.

For the first time tanks accompanied the storming waves, giving the enemy an unpleasant surprise, which contributed largely to the victory.

In the centre, the tanks entered Flers before noon; the troops advanced beyond the village and established themselves. On the left, Foureaux Wood, bristling with strong-points and redoubts, and on the right, Hill 154 were carried, and the Morval—Lesbœufs—Gueudecourt line reached.

In consequence of this brilliant success of the British right, the attack was extended on the left; the tanks entered Martinpuich and Courcelette. In a single day the British advanced 2 km. along a 10 km. front, and captured 4,000 prisoners.

The enemy threw two more divisions into the battle, and fiercely counter-attacked the salient formed by the French lines at the Bapaume-Péronne road. After getting a footing in Bouchavesnes on September 20, they were driven out at the point of the bayonet.

The General Attack of September 25, and Capture of Combles

The Allied front line moved forward again, to complete the investment of Combles.

Rancourt and Frégicourt fell on the 25th, in the French attack; Morval was captured by the British.

The encirclement of Combles was complete, and the enemy had already partially evacuated the place. On the 26th, the British entered the fortress from the north, the French from the south, and captured a company of laggards.

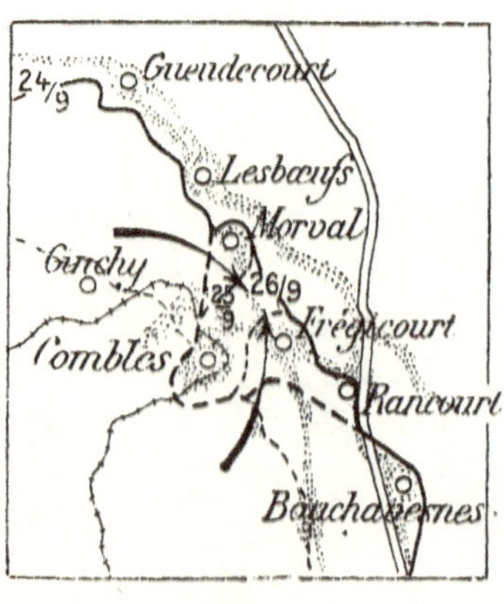

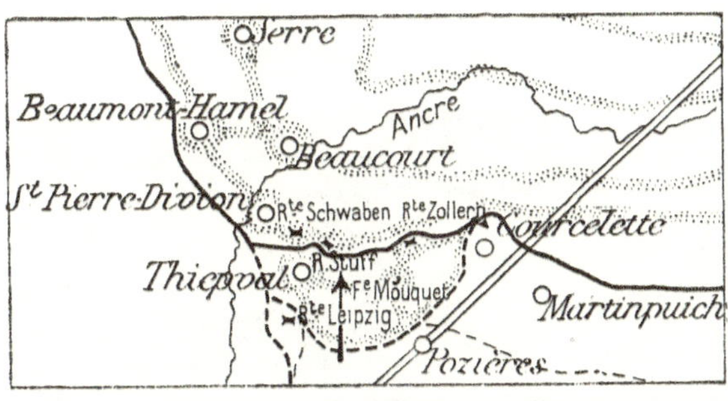

The Turning and Capture of Thiepval Plateau

West of the lines of the 4th British Army, and dominating the valley of the Ancre, the powerfully fortified Thiepval Plateau still remained uncaptured. This very strong system of defences comprised the village, Mouquet Farm, and the Zollern, Schwaben and Stuff Redoubts.

In July, the British had gained a footing in the Leipzig Redoubt, which formed the first enemy positions south of the Plateau. In August, Pozières had been carried by the Australians. On September 15, the British captured Martinpuich and Courcelette, and progressed beyond the plateau to the east.

The Attack of September 26

On September 26, the day Combles was taken, an attack was made against this formidable plateau. Mouquet Farm and Zollern Redoubt fell, and on the 27th, Thiepval was captured (*see p. 48*).

The British carried the trenches connecting the Schwaben and Stuff Redoubts, but the enemy still clung to the northern slopes of the plateau which descends towards the Ancre.

The Attack of November 13

The German lines now formed a sharp salient on the Ancre.

To reduce this salient and complete the capture of Thiepval Plateau, the British attacked on both sides of the river.

The attack was delivered in a thick fog, on the 13th, when St. Pierre-Division and Beaumont-Hamel fell; the same evening Beaucourt village was encircled, to be captured on the morrow. On the following days, the assailants successfully resisted numerous counter-attacks. From the 13th to the 19th, 7,000 prisoners were taken, and the whole of Thiepval Plateau was captured.

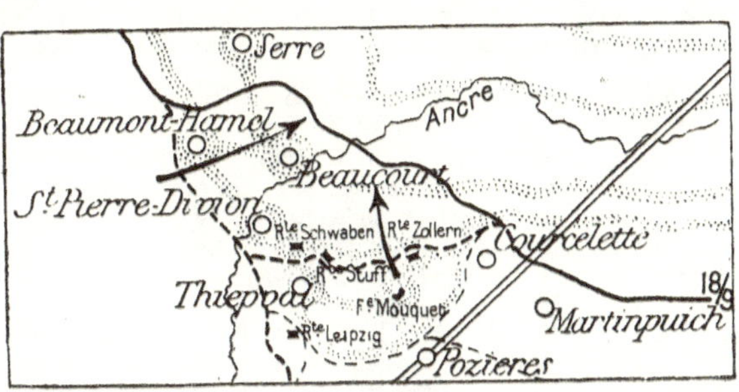

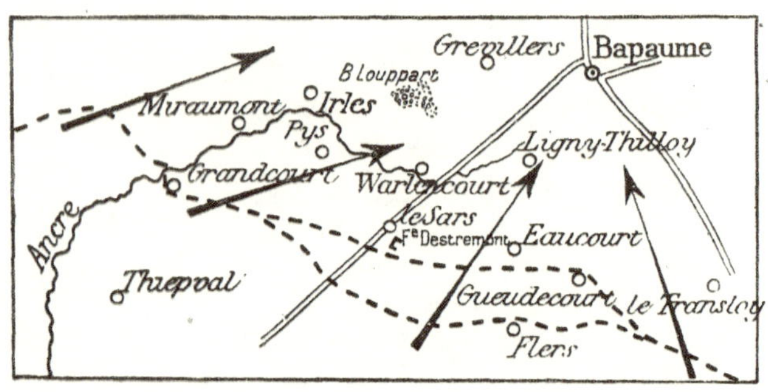

The Advance towards the Main Objectives (Bapaume—Péronne)

Towards Bapaume.—The British advance on the two wings—Thiepval to the west and Gueudecourt to the east—forced the German centre back on the Le Sars-Eaucourt line. Continuing to press the enemy, the British carried Destremont Farm, in front of Le Sars, on September 29, while on October 3, the village of Eaucourt-l'Abbaye was taken. On the 7th, a further advance was made along the spur which forms a salient in front of Le Transloy village, and Le Sars village was carried the same day.

A single line of heights only now separated the British Army from Bapaume, 6 km. distant from Le Sars. This line consisted chiefly of Warlencourt Ridge, which dominates the country all round, and which had been turned by the Germans into an apparently impregnable fortress.

Although the bad weather and the mud now forced the Allies to suspend their offensive, sharp fighting continued. From December to the end of January the British raided the enemy's trenches unceasingly.

After that, operations were resumed to reduce the Ancre salient completely. The improvement, realised since the previous summer, in their offensive strength, at once became apparent. Their artillery, reinforced, thoroughly "pounded" the whole terrain, making it possible for the infantry to force a way through all obstacles, and to advance continuously.

Advancing over the tops of the hills, which border the Upper Ancre, the British directed their efforts alternately against both banks of the river, and soon rendered untenable those positions still held by the Germans at the bottom of the valleys. On February 7, 1917, Grandcourt was captured, while the week following, Miraumont, Pys, Warlencourt with its famous Ridge, and Ligny-Thilloy (within 3 km. of Bapaume) were surrounded.

The Germans now fell back on a new line of defences close to the town, and by strong counter-attacks sought to stay the British advance. Their efforts were in vain, however, and the British hemmed them in more closely each day. Irles was occupied on March 10 ; Louppart Wood and Grévillers on the 13th. On the 14th, the British were at the gates of Bapaume, which they entered three days later (the 17th), only to find that the town had been burnt and methodically destroyed by the Germans.

Towards Péronne.—On October 1, the French lines, in *liaison* with those of the British south of Morval, took in Rancourt, Bouchavesnes and Labbé Farm, passed in front of Feuillancourt and reached the Somme at Omiécourt.

After a halt, devoted to the consolidation of the ground, the French resumed their advance, in spite of the bad weather. The objective was now to widen the positions beyond the Bapaume-Péronne road, in order to turn the town from the north, as the marshes of the Somme and the defences of Mont-Saint-Quentin did not permit a frontal attack.

On October 7, the road was occupied from Rancourt to within about 200 yards of the first houses of Sailly-Saillisel, and the western and south-western outskirts of Saint-Pierre-Vaast Wood were reached. During the following weeks the fighting, which was furious, concentrated around Sailly-Saillisel. On October 18, Sailly was carried, but Saillisel held out until the beginning of November. Meanwhile, the French made several unsuccessful attempts to carry the defence-works of Saint-Pierre-Vaast Wood, and finally remained hanging on to the western outskirts, in close contact with the enemy.

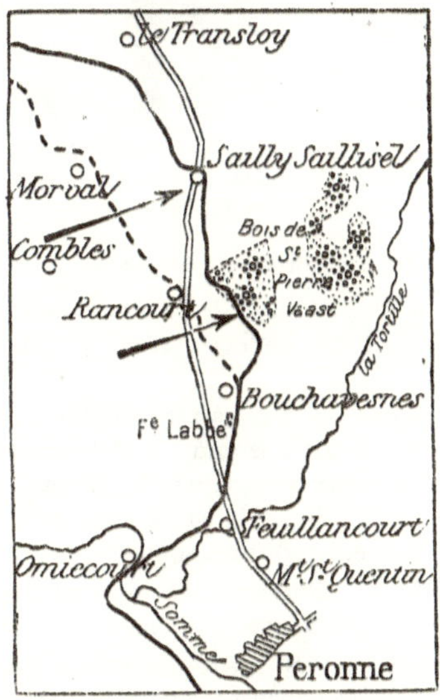

At the end of 1916, the front line in this sector extended from the northern outskirts of Sailly-Saillisel, along the western edges of Saint-Pierre-Vaast Wood, then took in Bouchavesnes and crossed the Somme near Omiécourt.

The winter passed quietly, except in the region of Sailly-Saillisel and Saint-Pierre-Vaast Wood, where skirmishing and grenade fighting were incessant. The British took possession of the sector and fortified it strongly, raiding from time to time the enemy trenches.

In March, 1917, the artillery duel increased in intensity, and the Germans prepared to evacuate their positions.

Their retreat began on March 15, after the country had been methodically devastated. The British occupied the whole wood of Saint-Pierre-Vaast on the 15th and 16th, almost without striking a blow. On the 17th, they held the Mont-Saint-Quentin—powerful advance fortress of Péronne. On the 18th, they finally entered the town from the north, while other detachments reached it from the south-east, across the marshes of the Somme.

PRESIDENT POINCARÉ HANDING THE "COMMANDEUR DE LA LÉGION D'HONNEUR" INSIGNIA TO GENERAL MICHELER.

The Battle of Attrition, South of the Somme

In the early days of July, in the diversion section south of the Somme, the French 1st Colonial Corps, having carried the three German positions, faced south-east.

The French lines, resting on the western outskirts of Omiécourt, followed the Somme Canal, encircled Biaches and La Maisonnette, turned south-west, and passed in front of Barleux village, which, hidden in a depression of the ground, had till then successfully resisted all assaults. The lines ran towards Soyécourt (still held by the enemy), then southwards *via* Lihons and Maucourt.

From La Maisonnette to Maucourt, they formed the sides of an enormous obtuse angle, the apex of which was Soyécourt.

The objective of the French 10th Army (General Micheler), disposed along the sides of this angle, was to widen the latter by means of continued thrusts in the direction of the southern end of the bend in the Somme. Its advance being then stayed by the important stronghold of Chaulnes, the latter was to be half-encircled, thereby seriously threatening the rear of the German positions south of the town.

The French offensive was launched on September 4. The outskirts of Deniécourt and Berny were reached in the first rush ; in the centre, Soyécourt was carried ; on the left, Vermandovillers was partly captured and Chilly passed by about half a mile.

On the 5th, the Germans counter-attacked unsuccessfully, and failed to stay the French advance. On the 6th, half the village of Berny was taken. In three days, 6,650 prisoners and 36 guns, including 28 heavies, were captured.

A fresh offensive was combined, with the attack of the 12th by the Franco-British troops north of the Somme, and that of the 15th by the British troops operating beyond Combles.

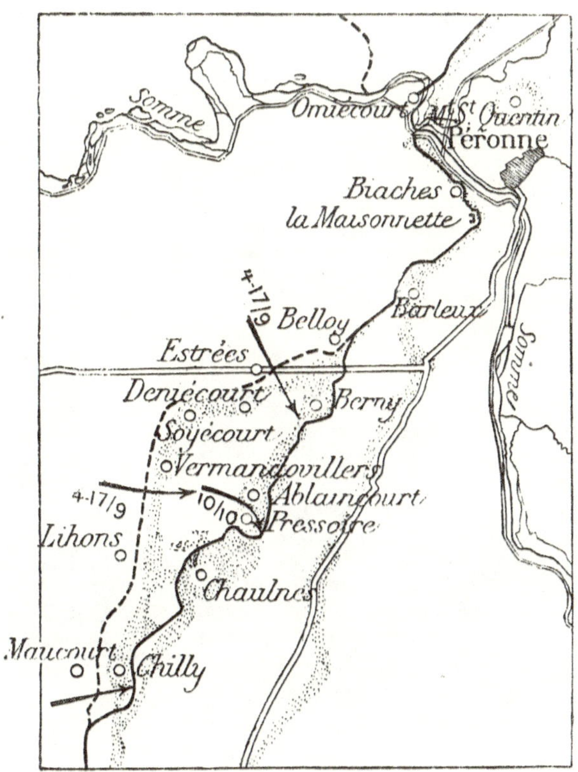

On the 17th, the conquest of Vermandovillers and Berny was completed, and on the 18th, the village of Deniécourt was encircled and captured.

On October 10th, the offensive was resumed after a heavy bombardment between Berny and Chaulnes. The hamlet of Bovent, north of Ablaincourt, was conquered, together with the western edge of Chaulnes Wood. Parts of these woods were captured in October, and at the beginning of November. The villages of Ablaincourt and Pressoire were also occupied.

Thanks to this slow but continuous advance, and to the capture of these various villages, the fortress of Chaulnes was outflanked and half-encircled.

However, the Germans managed to maintain themselves there, and the French progress was held in this sector, as it had been further north, by the stronghold of Barleux and the marshes of the Somme.

At the end of 1916, the front line of the sector south of the Somme started from Omiécourt, left Barleux in German hands, and crossed the Maisonnette Plateau. From there, it described a large circle *via* Berny (French) and Chaulnes (German), skirting Roye and Lassigny (*see sketch map, p.* 29).

The German Retreat of March, 1917

Although the Somme offensive did not give immediate strategical results, it nevertheless procured the Allies tactical advantages which were one of the causes of the German retreat of March, 1917.

The capture of important points of support made the position of the Germans a very precarious one, at all the points where they had so far succeeded in maintaining themselves. They feared that if in 1917 the Allies resumed their offensive—which the experience acquired in 1916 would render still more formidable—further retreat, resulting in the piercing of their front line, might become necessary. They consequently decided voluntarily to shorten their lines by falling back on new positions in the rear, known as the Hindenburg Line " (see the Michelin Guide: " THE HINDENBURG LINE ").

THE BAND OF THE AUSTRALIAN 5TH BRIGADE PASSING THROUGH THE SMOKING RUINS OF BAPAUME ON MARCH 19, 1917, WHILE THE BATTLE STILL RAGED NEAR BY, ON THE LINE BECQUINCOURT —NOVAINS.

The formation of a new defensive front was only possible by evacuating a large area, and the German retreat extended to the whole of the region comprised between Arras and Soissons. It was very skilfully carried out, unhampered by the Allies, who contented themselves with following close behind the retreating enemy.

On March 15 and 16, 1917, the French, informed by their Air Service of the enemy's imminent retirement, made numerous raids into the German trenches between the Oise and the Avre, advancing in places as much as 4 km. On the 17th, the cavalry, followed by the infantry, entered Lassigny and Roye. Noyon was occupied early on the 18th.

On the same day (March 17) the British, having relieved the French as far as south of Chaulnes during the winter, captured La Maisonnette, Barleux, Villers-Carbonnel and all the villages still occupied by the enemy within the loop of the Somme. On the 18th, they entered Péronne and Chaulnes.

The whole region between the Somme and the Oise was liberated at that time, after thirty months of German occupation, but only after it had been systematically and totally devastated, according to elaborate plans drawn up beforehand. These destructions were absolutely unjustifiable from a military point of view. Towns and villages were wiped out, houses plundered, industries ruined, factories destroyed, land devastated, agricultural implements broken, farms burnt, trees cut down—in a word, everything done to turn the place into "*a desert incapable for a long time of producing the things necessary to life*" (Berliner Tagblatt).

It was from these new lines that in the spring of the following year the Germans launched their great offensive, designed to separate the Allied armies and resume their march "*nach Paris.*"

The German offensive and the Allied counter-offensive of 1918 are dealt with in the Michelin Guide: "THE SECOND BATTLE OF THE SOMME (1918)."

In addition to the pushing back of the enemy front, the Allies' three immediate objectives had been attained.

Verdun was soon relieved of the German pressure, as the enemy "were exhausted and compelled to use their reserves for the Russian front, and especially in the Somme. Their activities on the Verdun front were limited to making good their losses. However, they were finally obliged to weaken this front to a point that they were unable to reply to the French attacks." (See the Michelin Guide: "VERDUN, AND THE BATTLES FOR ITS POSSESSION.")

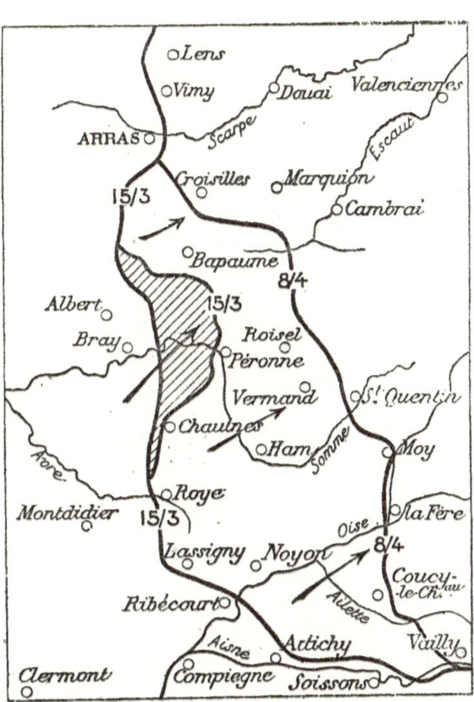

THE SHADED PORTION REPRESENTS THE GROUND CONQUERED DURING THE 1916–1917 OFFENSIVE.

The Allies' further aim to keep the maximum of the German forces on the western front was likewise attained. According to Field-Marshal Haig's report, the transfer of enemy troops from west to east, begun after the Russian offensive of June, lasted a very little time after the beginning of the Somme offensive. Afterwards, with one exception, the enemy only sent exhausted battle-worn divisions to the eastern front, which were always replaced by fresh divisions. In November, the number of enemy divisions present on the western front was greater than in July, in spite of the abandonment of the offensive against Verdun.

As regards the wearing down of the enemy's fighting strength, their losses in men and material were much heavier than those of the Allies.

Half the German forces in France came out of the battle physically and morally worn.

From July 1 to December 1, the enemy had more than 700,000 men put out of action (killed, wounded or prisoners). More than 300 guns were captured and many others destroyed.

The German nation, badly shaken by the violence and duration of the battle, alarmed at the events on the eastern front, and cruelly disappointed by their failure before Verdun, were on the point of suing for peace at the end of the Battles of the Somme.

On the other hand, the British had gained full consciousness of their strength, and had fought in closer union with their French comrades.

The Allies of all ranks had learned to know and appreciate one another better, and future operations were destined to become more closely co-ordinated. " To fight under such conditions unity of command is generally essential, but in this case, the cordial good feeling of the Allied Armies, and their sincere desire to help one another, served the same purpose and removed all difficulties " (Field-Marshal Haig).

Among the French, the veterans and young classes vied with one another in heroism. Many " *bleuets* " (twenty-year old youths) were under fire for the first time. In contact with their seasoned Verdun comrades, they fought with splendid dash. After scaling the craggy slopes east of Curlu village, many of them waved their handkerchiefs to cries of " *Vive la France !* "

Up to the middle in the foul Somme mud, which at times forced the men out of the trenches into the open, in spite of the shells and bullets, the Allied troops acquired the *morale* of Victory, while the High Command gained and kept the initiative.

GERMAN TANK CAPTURED BY THE NEW ZEALANDERS
DURING THE ALLIED OFFENSIVE OF 1918.
Extracted from the Michelin Guide " THE SECOND BATTLE OF THE SOMME (1918)

A VISIT TO THE SOMME BATTLEFIELDS.

FIRST DAY.

AMIENS—ALBERT—THIEPVAL—BAPAUME.

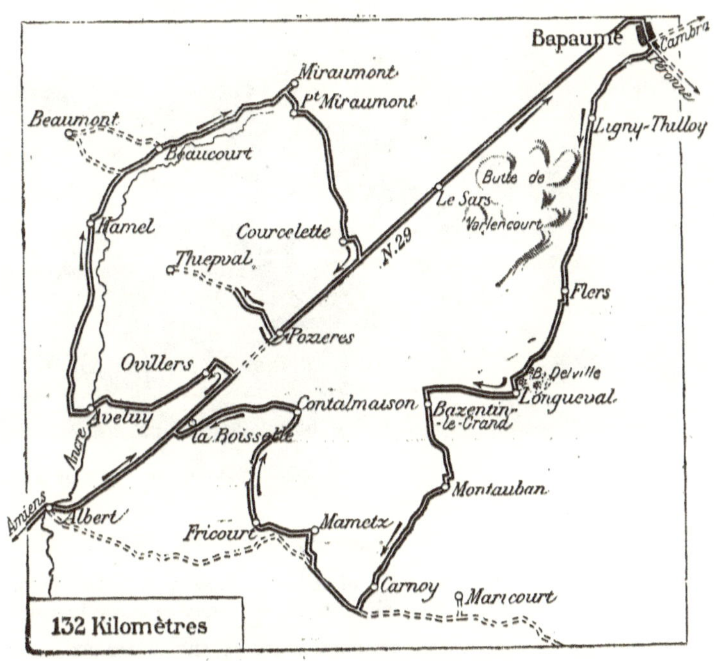

ITINERARY FOR THE FIRST DAY.

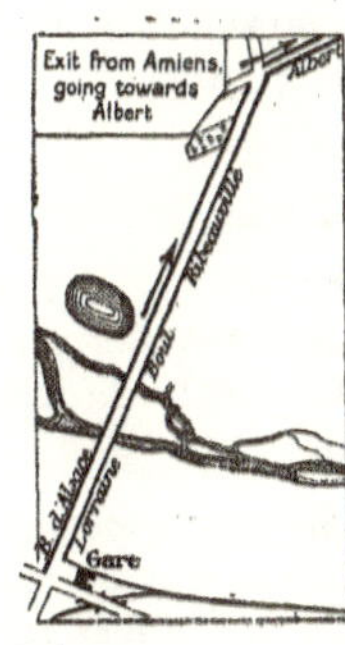

Leave **Amiens** *by the Boulevard d'Alsace-Lorraine, in front of the station, on the left. Beyond the cemetery, take N. 29 to Albert, on the right.*

Eleven kilometres beyond Amiens, **Pont-Noyelles** *is passed through.* This village was made famous by the sanguinary, indecisive battle fought there on December 23, 1870, between the French and Germans. To the left of the road, just outside the village, a monument commemorates the battle.

Twenty-eight kilometres beyond Amiens, N. 29 enters **Albert.**

PANORAMIC VIEW OF ALBERT, AS SEEI

ALBERT.

The prosperous, industrial town of Albert, whose population before the war numbered more than 7,000 inhabitants, is to-day entirely in ruins.

Lying at the foot of a hill, on both sides of the River Ancre, Albert formerly went by the name of Ancre.

At the beginning of the seventeenth century Albert belonged to Concini, the favourite minister of Marie de Medicis, but after his downfall in 1619 it became the property of Charles d'Albert, Duke of Luynes, who gave it his name.

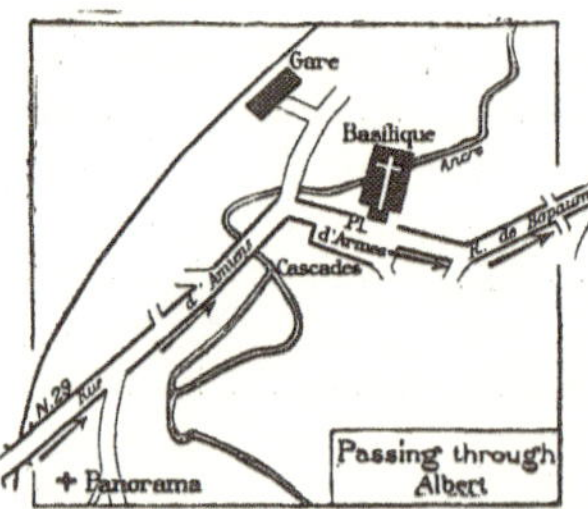

Albert during the War

When, after the first Battle of the Marne, the front advanced northwards, the Germans tried on several occasions to break through the French lines before Albert.

Fierce fighting took place in the immediate vicinity of the town at the end of September, 1914, especially on the 29th, and in October and

Boisselle
[ill.   G.C. 52.

ON ENTERING THE TOWN. (*See sketch, p.* 32.)

November. The Germans were repulsed with heavy losses, but succeeded in entrenching themselves strongly quite close to the city, and barred the Albert-Bapaume road (N. 29) to the north-east, in front of La Boisselle and the Albert-Péronne road, in front of Fricourt.

The shelling of the town began on September 29, 1914, and continued unceasingly until it had been annihilated. The numerous iron and steel works, mechanical workshops, sugar factories and brick-kilns, which had contributed to the prosperity of the town, were specially singled out by the enemy artillery. No public building, not excepting the civilian hospital, was spared. In spite of the Red Cross flag which floated over the hospital, the Germans, with the help of an aeroplane, directed a violent artillery fire upon it on March 21, 1915, killing five aged inmates and wounding several others, as well as the Superior.

In October, 1916, Albert was at last out of range of the German guns.

But in 1918 the British were unable to withstand the overwhelming German thrust, except on the west of the town, and the latter fell into the hands of the enemy on March 26, after desperate fighting. Albert remained in the first enemy lines until August 22, when the British counter-offensive, which was destined to clear the whole district—this time definitely—was launched. The British entered the town in the early morning of August 22.

ALBERT CHURCH IN APRIL, 1917.

A Visit to the Ruins—The Basilica

Arriving by the Rue d'Amiens, tourists will see the cascade, *on the right behind a* ruined factory.

ALBERT CHURCH IN 1919.

RUINED WORKS ON RIVER ANCRE, AND CASCADE.

Follow the Rue d'Amiens to the Place d'Armes, in which stand the ruins of the **Church of Nôtre-Dame-de-Brebière.** Before the war as many as 80,000 people made pilgrimages to this basilica yearly, to see the ancient statue of the Virgin, discovered in the neighbourhood by a shepherd, in the Middle-Ages.

The church—a brick-and-stone construction in the Roman-Byzantine style—was built at the end of the nineteenth century. The brick belfry, over 200 feet high, was surmounted by a copper dome, on which stood a gilt statue of the Virgin, sixteen feet high, with the infant Jesus in her outstretched arms. The body of the church measured 276 feet in length and 68 feet in height, and was very richly decorated.

The church was spared by the first bombardments, on account of two spies who, hidden in the top of the tower, made signals to the Germans, but as soon as they had been discovered and shot, the church became a target for the enemy artillery. The walls of the façade soon showed large gaps in many places. The roof fell in and the belfry was badly damaged, especially on the south side. A shell struck the top of the dome and burst against the socle of the statue of the Virgin. The base gave way, but did not entirely collapse, and the statue overturning remained suspended in mid-air (*photo, p. 34*).

For several years the statue remained in this precarious position, and there was a saying that " the war would end when the Virgin Statue of Albert would fall."

The bombardments in the spring of 1918 completed the ruin of the church. Not only did the belfry collapse, carrying in its fall the statue of the Virgin, but all the upper structure which had until then resisted, fell down, so that to-day the immense building is a shapeless heap of stones, bricks and *débris* of all kinds (*photo, p. 34*).

LA BOISSELLE.   THE SIGN IS ALL THAT REMAINS OF
THE VILLAGE.

*Leave Albert by the Rue de Bapaume, then take N. 29 which climbs La Bois-
selle Hill.   2 km. beyond Albert there is a large cemetery on the right.*   The
site of Boisselle village (completely destroyed) *is reached 2 km. further on.*

The Mine Warfare at La Boisselle

In October, 1914, the front line became fixed, west of this village.   A
fierce trench-to-trench struggle continued throughout 1915, when it developed
into ceaseless, desperate mine warfare.

At the end of December, 1914, the French captured that part of La
Boisselle which lies south of the church.   German counter-attacks, launched
almost daily, failed to drive them out.   On January 17, 1915, after a violent
bombardment, the French were compelled to withdraw from that corner
of the hamlet, but the next day they succeeded in re-occupying the still
smoking ruins.

These attacks and counter-attacks had brought the German and French
trenches so close together that it became impossible to fight in the open.
The struggle was therefore continued underground.   On both sides subterranean galleries were bored under the opposing trenches, generally to a
depth of 20 to 26 feet.   Mine-chambers, filled with cheddite, at the end of
the galleries, were fired electrically.   In the ensuing upheaval the trenches
entirely disappeared, giving place to huge craters, for the possession of the
edges of which bitter hand-to-hand fighting followed.

BRITISH CEMETERY, BETWEEN ALBERT AND LA BOISSELLE,
ON THE RIGHT.

During the night of February 6, 1915, the Germans fired three mines in the southern part of La Boisselle occupied by the French, and captured the craters, but were unable to debouch from them. The next day a spirited French counter-attack drove them back.

The communiqués of 1915 mention many feats of this kind, and to-day the traces which still remain of this ferocious struggle attest its extreme violence.

On each side of the Albert-Bapaume road, opposite La Boisselle village, huge craters form an almost continuous line.

The largest crater lies on the right. It has a diameter of about 200 feet and a depth of 81 feet. British graves lie at the bottom (*photo opposite*).

This mine warfare procured no appreciable advantage to either side.

BRITISH GRAVES IN THE GREAT MINE CRATER AT LA BOISSELLE.

Fresh defences were immediately made on the edge of or near the new craters, in place of those which had been wiped out, and the front line remained practically unchanged until the offensive of the Somme.

On July 1, 1916, the British rushed the German trenches in front of La Boisselle and Ovillers, giving rise to a fierce engagement. After two days of incessant fighting the whole of La Boisselle village was captured. A battalion of the Prussian Guard made a desperate resistance at Ovillers, the survivors—124 men and 2 officers—surrendering only on July 17.

MINE CRATER AT LA BOISSELLE.

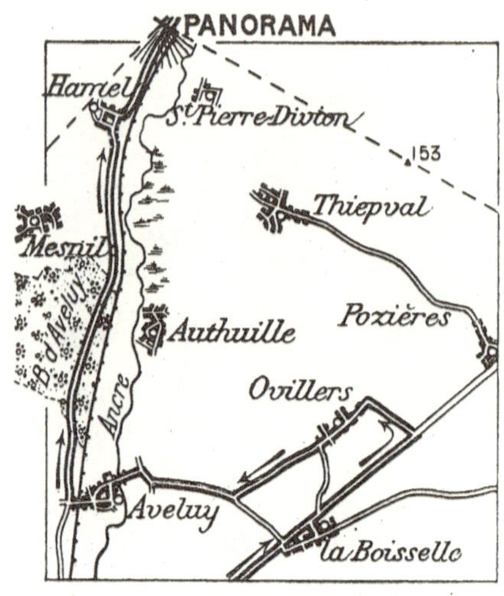

Leave La Boisselle on the right, and take N. 29.

Ten yards from milestone "Albert 5 km. 4," take the left-hand road to **Ovillers** *(600 yards distant).* Of this village not a wall remains standing.

The road turns to the left and crosses the village, in which numerous shelters and military works can still be seen.

Outside Ovillers, on the right, there is a large cross, erected by the British in memory of their fallen comrades of the 12th Division. *A little further on, there is* a British cemetery *on the same side of the road.*

The road turns to the right, then descends steeply to the Ancre marshes. Cross these by the footbridge built by the Army Engineers, to **Aveluy** *village on the opposite side.*

Of this village, only a few walls remain standing, among which are numerous military works.

On leaving Aveluy, the road crosses the railway. Take the road on the right immediately after.

Follow the marshy valley of the Ancre upstream.

Hill 153. St. Pierre-Divion. Thiepval.

PANORAMIC VIEW OF THE VALLEY OF THE ANCRE, AS SEEN

THE ANCRE MARSHES, IN FRONT OF THE RUINS OF AVELUY.

The road crosses **Aveluy Wood,** *the trees of which are cut to pieces.
2 km. 500 beyond Aveluy, before the fork with the road to Mesnil, there is a*
British cemetery *on the right.*
On leaving the wood, follow the railway to the ruins of **Hamel** village. *Before
entering,* note the British cemetery *on the left.*
Opposite, on the crest of the hill, on the left bank of the Ancre, is **Thiepval
Wood,** cut to pieces by the shells. The view of the Ancre Valley from here is
most impressive (*photo below*).

Ancre Marshes.	Albert Arras Ry.	Albert.		Aveluy Wood.	G.C. 50.	Mesnil.	Hamel (behind crest)

ꞋN LEAVING HAMEL FOR BEAUCOURT-SUR-ANCRE.

The British Operations in the Ancre Sector

During the first months of the offensive of 1916, the Germans, installed on the top of the slopes which dominate both banks of the river, resisted successfully in the Ancre sector. On the east, they occupied the whole of the Thiepval Plateau (maximum altitude, 540 feet), which they transformed into a veritable fortress. To the west, after crossing the Ancre below the hamlet of St.-Pierre-Divion, their trenches ran in front of the high ground of Beaumont-Hamel (Hill 135) and Serre (Hills 143 and 141). From these elevated points they dominated the British positions, which is why the British, before attacking, were forced to take the Thiepval Ridge (end of September, 1916). This enabled them to take the German intrenchments in the rear.

On November 13, 1916, the attack was launched under very unfavourable weather conditions. The ground was sodden, and a thick fog hid everything from view. In spite, however, of the five successive lines of trenches which protected the enemy positions, the British first captured the hamlet of St.-Pierre-Divion, then, three hours afterwards, the fortress of Beaumont.

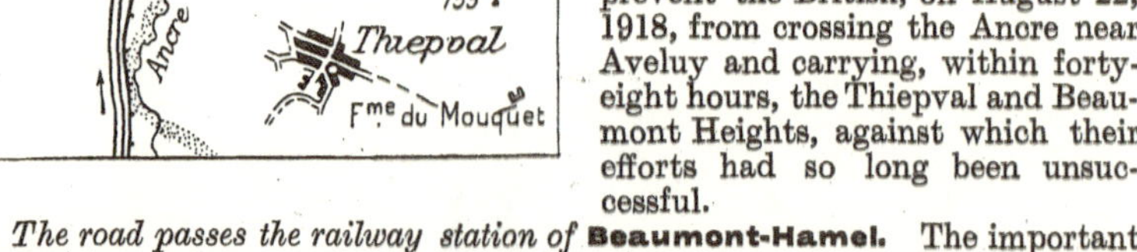

In 1918, the German thrust broke down, as in 1914, on the banks of the Ancre. Caught in the swampy ground, they were unable to establish themselves strongly on the heights of the western bank. Leaving advanced posts only in the valley, with strong patrols, they re-occupied their old entrenched positions ; but with the ground in such a state of upheaval, a prolonged resistance there was impossible.

The Germans were unable to prevent the British, on August 22, 1918, from crossing the Ancre near Aveluy and carrying, within forty-eight hours, the Thiepval and Beaumont Heights, against which their efforts had so long been unsuccessful.

The road passes the railway station of **Beaumont-Hamel.** The important market town of this name (1 *km.* 500 *beyond the station*) is now a mere heap of chaotic ruins.

The report of the Enquiry Commission appointed by the French Government, contains the following :—

" *On October 12, 1914, an aeroplane flew over Beaumont-Hamel. The Germans pretended that two women (Mme. Roussel and Mme. Flament) signalled to the aeroplane, the first-named by leading a red horse and a white horse into her yard, the second woman by displaying a large piece of cloth-stuff. The facts are : Mme. Flament had simply used her handkerchief, and Mme. Roussel, in the absence of her mobilised husband, having to attend to their large farm, had led two horses into the yard, to facilitate the cleaning of the stable.*

" *Together with other inhabitants of the village who were under arrest for similar futile motives, Mme. Roussel and Mme. Flament were questioned by*

BEAUMONT-HAMEL, WHERE THE CHURCH USED TO STAND.

the officer attached to the Colonel commanding the 110th Infantry Regiment. After having ordered them to confess their guilt, this officer was particularly infuriated against Mme. Flament, and promised the others that their lives should be spared if they would denounce her. He had a personal grievance against the woman. A few days before he had asked her for champagne wine, and she had replied that she had not any, but, on leaving the house, he noticed that some of his men had wine and, believing that she had mocked him, he had indulged in violent reproaches.

" In spite of the danger, the brave women replied that they preferred to die rather than accuse an innocent person. Exasperated by their resistance, the German allowed them three minutes for reflection, and then had them placed against the wall of the church. While his soldiers covered the women with their rifles, he counted, ' one, two——,' then, in the belief that this sham execution had terrorized the defenceless women, he allowed them half an hour's respite and sent them back to the Town Hall. At the expiration of this delay he again pressed them with questions, seized two sums of money (one of 776 francs, the other of 1,345 francs, which Mme. Roussel and Mme. Flament, believing that their last hour had come, had requested a friend to hand over to their families), threatened in a fit of rage to have Mme. Flament buried alive, and ordered all the persons under arrest to swear that they were innocent. At the last moment, the courage to carry out this abomination failed him, and he sent the unfortunate women back to Mme. Roussel's house. Here they were watched until October 28, and were then sent to Cambrai with the other inhabitants who had been held as hostages, because they were unable to pay the whole of the war contribution of 8,000 francs which had been set upon the district."—Report of December 8, 1915, page 22, Vol. V.

One kilometre beyond the station of Beaucourt-Hamel the road crosses the village of **Beaucourt,** *where not a single wall remains standing (see sketch-map, p. 40).*

It was on November 13, 1916, that the British, after capturing Beaumont-Hamel, carried Hill No. 135, between Beaumont and Beaucourt, and reached the outskirts of Beaucourt. The entire village was occupied the next day.

But the approaching winter and continuous bad weather did not allow them to exploit their success. In the operations of the previous two days, they had been greatly hampered by the deep sticky mud through which, in places, the men had had to advance up to their waists. It was therefore decided to make the new positions their winter quarters.

The cessation of the offensive did not, however, mean inaction. From November, 1916, to the end of January, 1917, raids were incessantly carried out in the enemy trenches.

Early in February, 1917, a violent and incessant bombardment was the forerunner of fresh attacks. From February 8 onwards, the British made considerable progress along the Beaucourt-Miraumont road.

After leaving Beaucourt, keep along this road. A great heap of red bricks, on the right, by the side of the river Ancre, is all that remains of Baillescourt Farm, the defence-works of which were captured on February 8, 1917.

A few days later, the British reached the outskirts of the important position of **Miraumont.**

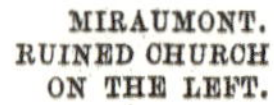

MIRAUMONT.
RUINED CHURCH
ON THE LEFT.

This large village was divided by the Ancre and the Albert-Arras railway, the village proper being situated on the north bank. The smaller agglomeration of houses lying on the south bank, known as Petit-Miraumont, was the first to fall into the hands of the British, after desperate fighting. The approaches to Petit-Miraumont had been covered with successive lines of trenches, bristling with barbed wire entanglements, redoubts and concrete blockhouses for machine-guns. All these positions had to be carried one by one. The village itself was only captured on February 24, 1917.

Two days later, Miraumont-le-Grand, defended only by a rearguard company and a section of machine-gunners, was easily carried by the British. This marked the beginning of the "strategical withdrawal" which, the following month, ended with the capture of Bapaume, Miraumont (7 km. to the west) being one of its advance fortresses.

Lost again in the following year, Miraumont was one of the few positions which the Germans fiercely defended at the time of the British counter-offensive of August, 1918. They tried all they knew to stop the British advance on Bapaume at this point. The fight lasted all day on August 24, and the German retirement began only after the capture of Grandcourt and Thiepval (on the south) and of Irles and Loupart Wood (on the north-east) threatened them with complete encirclement. That night, a strong detachment of British troops slipped into the fortified ruins of the village, held by picked machine-gunners. A fierce struggle followed in the dark. At daybreak the German garrison attempted a sortie, and succeeded in encircling the British detachments. However, a British aeroplane, which was hovering over the scene of the struggle, signalled that reinforcements were coming, and finally the Germans were encircled, and several hundreds of them taken prisoners.

After the fights of 1916, Miraumont was one of the least damaged of the reconquered villages. Many of the houses retained parts of their walls, and some their framework, though in a dislocated condition. To-day nothing remains. Of the modern church which used to stand on the highest point of the village, only a fragment of wall

GERMAN MONUMENT IN FRONT OF MIRAUMONT CHURCH (1917).

remains (*photo, p. 42*). On the right, in the devastated cemetery which surrounds the church, stands a massive stone monument, erected by the Germans before their retreat of 1917 (*photos, above and below*).

At the entrance to Miraumont, take the Courcelette road on the right, which crosses the marshes, then passes under the railway bridge and afterwards traverses the site of Petit-Miraumont (now razed). It next climbs the hill on the left bank of the Ancre. Leave the road to Pys on the left, and keep straight on to **Courcelette.** Numerous shelters, trenches and British and German graves may be seen along the road.

The village of Courcelette was taken by the British during the offensive of September 15, 1916.

MIRAUMONT. RUINS OF CHURCH AND GERMAN MONUMENT (1918—*see above*).

MIRAUMONT.   BRITISH GRAVES IN FRONT
OF CHURCH.

(see p. 22)

THE BRITISH OFFENSIVE OF SEPTEMBER 15, 1916.

The First Tanks

The British objective was Courcelette, Martinpuich and the neighbouring heights which protected the Bapaume Plateau (*see p.* 22).

The offensive began on September 15, along a front of about six miles, from the neighbourhood of Combles to the trenches before Pozières.

In a few hours, the infantry, preceded in its advance by impassable artillery barrages, carried Martinpuich and the small hills which dominate it.   Other detachments captured Courcelette on the left.

The fighting was particularly

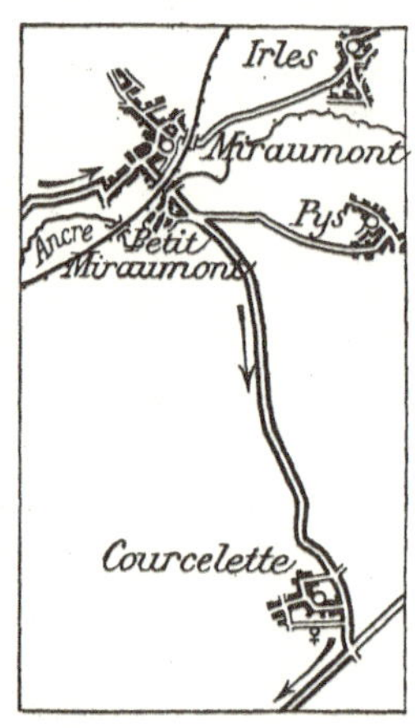

desperate before Courcelette.   The first two assaulting waves broke against the double line of enemy trenches, flanked by redoubts and salients armed with mortars and machine-guns.   Further artillery preparation was necessary, and it was only at nightfall that the Canadians were able to enter the village.   A tank immediately set about clearing the streets.

It was in this offensive that tanks were used for the first time, to the great disturbance of the enemy's *morale*.

At Martinpuich they crushed down the walls which were still standing, and behind which machine-guns were hidden.

COURCELETTE.   ALL THAT IS LEFT OF THE CHURCH.

MARTINPUICH.   THE CHURCH USED TO STAND HERE.

One tank went for the fortified sugar factory in front of Courcelette village, knocked down the walls, crushed the numerous machine-guns hidden behind them, destroyed all the defence-works and quickly overcame the enemy's resistance.

On leaving Courcelette, take N. 29 on the right towards Pozières and Thiepval (see sketch-map, p. 44).

On the right of the road stand the ruins of a large sugar factory with a

BRITISH TANK BETWEEN COURCELETTE AND N. 29.

GERMAN OBSERVATION-POST OF CONCRETE,
IN THE ENGINE-ROOM.

concrete observation-post. *Further on, also to the right*, there is a cross erected by the British.

Before reaching Pozières, N. 29 passes over Hill 160. The windmill which formerly stood there has disappeared.

From the top of Hill 160, which dominates the whole district, there is an extensive view in the direction of Bapaume. To keep this observation-post, the Germans transformed Pozières into a fortress defended by more than 200 machine-guns.

After capturing Ovillers-la-Boisselle and advancing little by little along the National road as far as the outskirts of Pozières, the British attacked on July 23, 1916; but only at midnight were they able to get a footing in the village. Throughout the night and the two following days, the fighting went on with unabated fury. It was only on July 26 that the Germans were definitively driven from the northern part of the village, and the fortified cemetery, and a few days later from the windmill on Hill 160.

BRITISH CROSS. *In front :* OVERTURNED TANK.

POZIÈRES. GERMAN OBSERVATION-POST.

Violent counter-attacks were made in August, liquid fire being used in some cases. These attacks were particularly fierce to the north-west of the village and in the vicinity of the windmill, on the night of August 16, when six assaulting waves were broken by the British artillery barrage-fire.

When this furious struggle died down, nothing was left of the village. Its site, completely levelled and upturned, is now indistinguishable from the surrounding country—formerly fruitful fields of corn and beet, to-day a chaotic waste of shell-holes.

A German observation-post of concrete *is seen on the right*, and another, less damaged, with very deep shelters (*photo below*), *also on the right.*   *On leaving the village,* 300 *yards further on, to the right,* there is a large British cemetery.

In the village of Pozières, the road to Thiepval, which branches off to the right, is only passable for about 1 *km.* 500. *From this point the tourist should go on foot to Thiepval.*

POZIÈRES. GERMAN OBSERVATION-POST.

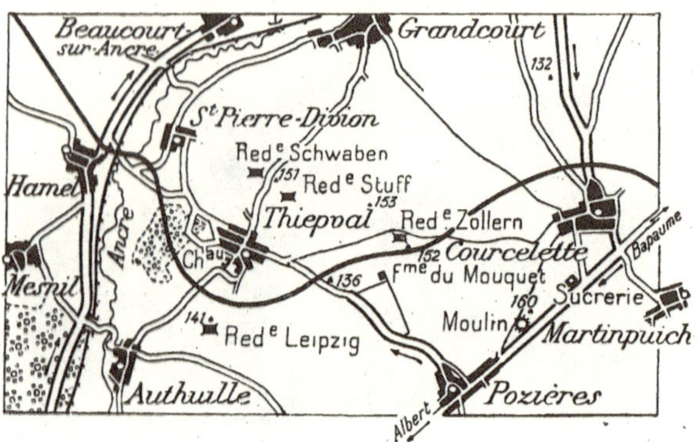

The Capture of Thiepval by the British

Situated on a plateau surrounded by hills, Thiepval had been transformed into a veritable fortress. Since September, 1914, the Wurtemburger 180th Regiment had been garrisoned there, and made it a point of honour to hold the place at all cost. For twenty months, formidable defence-works had been made; redoubts, blockhouses and concrete vaulted shelters, built on the surrounding high ground, formed a continuous, fortified line around the village. Inside, a labyrinth of trenches, connected by subterranean passages, linked up with strong points and to bombardment-proof shelters.

The British were forced to lay siege to the place. The operations, begun on July 3, 1916, lasted till October.

On July 7, the British carried the greater part of the Leipzig Redoubt (Hill 141), a powerful stronghold which protected Thiepval from the south, and consisting of a system of small blockhouses connected up by a network of trenches. A wide breach opened by the artillery, enabled the troops to gain a footing in the position and conquer it trench by trench.

Throughout the months of July and August the struggle went on, with unabated fury, around the fortress. Fighting with grenades, the British advanced inch by inch, so to speak, and eventually gained a footing in the village, to the east and south. Each advance was immediately followed by a violent counter-attack, as the Germans looked on Thiepval as the key of the Bapaume position.

On August 26, in particular, the Prussian Guard attacked the British lines of the Leipzig Salient. The struggle was one of " giants." After furious hand-to-hand fighting, the Wiltshire and Worcestershire Regiments broke the assaulting waves and inflicted " frightful " losses on the enemy. At no point were the British positions pierced; on the contrary, progress continued to the south and south-east.

On September 15, the Australians captured Mouquet Farm which, on the right, formed the advance-bastion of the fortress.

Thiepval was now completely surrounded from south to east, and after a last artillery preparation of extreme violence, the final assault was made.

At 12.30 a.m., on September 25, the Canadians attacked the castle and southern part of the village, one of the strongholds of the fortress. After fierce fighting, which lasted two hours, they captured the defence-works, being helped by the tanks which, crushing everything before them, destroyed the nests of machine-guns hidden on all sides.

The battle went on throughout the following day in the village, the cellars of which were connected with one another and fortified, forming so many nests of machine-guns. Detachments of Wurtembergers who, by means of underground passages, had slipped behind the Canadians, were either exterminated or captured. In the evening, the cemetery, which formed the centre of resistance in the northern part of the village, was carried. Thiepval was thus entirely conquered, as well as the Zollern Redoubt, which dominates it on the east.

The British followed up their success by attacking the fortified positions to the north and north-east, on the line of hills which dominate the Valley of the Ancre near Grandcourt, where the Germans had also made formidable entrenchments, comprising the Stuff Redoubt (to the north-east), the Schwaben Redoubt (to the north), and between the two, astride of the Thiepval-Grandcourt road (G.C. 151), the Hesse Trench. Behind these, in the direction of Grandcourt, the Shiff and Regina Trenches, likewise powerfully organised, formed a second line of entrenchments.

From September 27 to October 1, the fighting was bitter and incessant, both redoubts and the Hesse Trench changing hands several times. Finally, the British remained masters of these positions, but were afterwards held by the following trenches—the Shiff and Regina—to which they had to lay siege. Progress was very slow, in spite of incessant grenade fighting, and when winter arrived, they had not yet conquered the whole of these trenches.

THE RUINS OF THIEPVAL.

WHERE THE CHÂTEAU OF THIEPVAL USED TO STAND.

The recapture of the Thiepval Plateau by the Germans at the end of March, 1918, did not give rise to any important engagement, no special effort being made to defend it.   In the same way, it is said that when the British finally drove out the Germans a few months later (August 24, 1918), they did not lose a single man.

Everything was pounded to bits by the shells.   Of the one-time flourishing village, nothing remains.   A shapeless mass of broken stones marks the site of the Castle (*photo above*).   The place has become a desolate waste overrun with weeds and grass.   Here and there traces of the defence-works : redoubts, trenches, etc., and the graves of British and German soldiers, conjure up visions of the bloody struggle which took place there.

Return to Pozières, take again N. 29 on the left, towards Bapaume.

RUINS OF SARS VILLAGE.   N. 29 NEAR BAPAUME.

SARS. RUINS OF GERMAN MONUMENT IN CEMETERY ON
THE RIGHT OF N. 29.

Five kilometres beyond Pozières, **Sars,** *which stood on both sides of the high
road, is reached (photo, p. 50).*   It was taken on October 7, 1916, by the British,
who advanced beyond it, but were then held, as in spite of repeated assaults the
Germans had maintained themselves on the Warlencourt Ridge (Hill 122),
to the east, which dominates the whole district.

Sars is the nearest village to Bapaume, taken by the British in the course
of their offensive of 1916.   It was about 9 km. from their trenches (in front
of La Boisselle), and 6 km. this side of the first houses of Bapaume.   In 1918,
on the contrary, it took the British only three days to cross the strip of
ground, 7 km. wide, which separated their starting trenches from Le Sars
village, captured on August 25.

Sars was wiped out.   At the entrance, in a small shell-torn wood on the
right, are the remains of a German cemetery, completely devastated.   The
base of a German monument can still be seen (*photo above*).

Continue along N. 29 for about 1 km. beyond Sars; 150 *yards to the right,*
Warlencourt Ridge stands out.   *Go there on foot.*

SARS. A CHINESE CAMP.

Warlencourt Ridge

Warlencourt Ridge is as tragically famous in the British Army as the Mort-Homme is for their French comrades-in-arms.

From the top of Hill 122, the last before Bapaume, the view embraces the whole region, renowned for the battles fought before the town first in the Franco-German War (1871) and then forty-six years later (1917–18). At the foot of the ridge lies the ruined village of Ligny-Thilloy; to the right, on the sky-line, accumulations of stones and rubbish, the suburbs of Bapaume; on the left, the remains of Loupart Wood, and, behind, a few broken walls, all that is left of the village of Grévillers.

The ground was everywhere cut up with trenches and defence-works, to destroy which a terrific pounding by the artillery was necessary. Not a single square yard escaped the deluge of shells, the destruction being as complete as it was methodical. Of the trenches, which were levelled before the fighting proper began, practically only traces remain. The woods, turned into fortresses, have likewise vanished, only shapeless tree-stumps being left. The villages were razed to their very foundations.

As far as the eye can reach, nothing is seen but a chaotic waste patched here and there with weeds and rank grass. In places, vestiges of the ancient barbed wire entanglements, which overran the ground in all directions, are met with. These were so numerous that the guns could not entirely destroy them, but wide gaps were made through which the attacking waves forced their way.

The Warlencourt Ridge proper consists of two superimposed eminences :

WARLENCOURT
RIDGE, SOUTH
SIDE.

a bare plateau about two-thirds of a mile in width—now covered with graves—and a chalky shell-torn hillock, which was the centre of the German position.

Pierced with subterranean galleries, furrowed with several successive lines of trenches, surrounded by a triple belt of entrenchments bristling with barbed wire entanglements and flanked at every angle by redoubts with innumerable mortars and machine-guns, such was the ridge which, like an impregnable fortress, faced the British trenches throughout the winter of 1916–17.

Several times in October and November, 1916, the British endeavoured to carry the position, but each time their attacks failed against the formidable defences. Only on February 25, 1917, did they succeed in taking it, after a feint attack on the rear-guards, which were protecting the withdrawal of the German main forces.

In 1917, the British erected five large crosses on the top of the ridge in memory of the units which took part in the assaults of 1916.

After visiting Warlencourt Ridge, return to N. 29, along which continue to **Bapaume** (5 *km.*).

THE TOP OF
THE RIDGE.

BAPAUME. BRITISH TANKS IN THE SUBURB OF ARRAS.

BAPAUME.

Situated on the road of invasion, at the intersection of the highways leading to Amiens, Arras, Cambrai and Soissons, Bapaume, in the course of past centuries, was several times besieged, destroyed or plundered. The town dates from the early Middle-Ages, and owes its origin to a fortified Castle built at the exit of the immense Arrouaise Forest, which at that time extended from the Ancre to the Sambre, and was infested by robbers and cut-throats. Mention of this particularity is found in an eleventh century heroic poem " En Aroaise a mauvaise ripaille."

BAPAUME. THE RUE D'ARRAS, SEEN FROM THE PLACE FAIDHERBE.

Under the protection of the Castle, the town grew rapidly, and soon became an important city, made wealthy by the trading between France and Flanders. Conquered by Louis XI., it afterwards fell into the hands of the Spaniards, and was transformed into a fortified town by Charles Quint. Recaptured by Francis I., it was lost again, and retaken only in 1641. Several years later, the Treaty of the Pyrenees (1659) ceded it definitely to France.

Bapaume in 1917

Utilising the ruins around and inside the town, the Germans had built very strong lines of defences at short distances, one behind the other, and preceded by deep barbed wire entanglements. But after the capture on March 11–13, 1917, of Louppart Wood and Grévillers, west of Bapaume— the only village in the district, whose houses and roofs were practically intact—the British were masters of all the crests of the Bapaume Plateau, and encircled the town so closely from north to south, that the Germans decided not to defend the latter, in spite of the powerful defences which they had accumulated. Before withdrawing, they destroyed the trenches, devastated the entire district, set death-traps everywhere, stretched chains, connected with mines, across the roads and paths, and set fire to the shelters, etc.

Neither the destructions nor the companies of machine-gunners which were left behind as rear-guards could stop the British, who occupied Bapaume on March 17, 1917, while the fires lighted in the town by the Germans were still burning.

BAPAUME. THE PLACE FAIDHERBE.

Bapaume in 1918

Whereas, in 1917, the British captured Bapaume by a frontal attack, they retook the town in August, 1918, by a wide turning movement.

As early as August 24, the New Zealanders of General Byng's Army, after carrying Louppart Wood, reached Avesnes-les-Bapaume, one of the suburbs of the town. The next day they advanced beyond the Bapaume-Arras road, and on the 27th conquered Beugnâtre (5 km. north-east of Bapaume). The town was furthermore surrounded on the south by the capture of Warlencourt Ridge. Unable to hold out any longer, the Germans evacuated or set fire to the immense stores in the town.

THE HÔTEL-DE-VILLE, BEFORE THE WAR.

On the 29th, the Welsh and New Zealand troops fought their way across the suburbs before nightfall, and hoisted the British and French flags on the ruins of the Town Hall.

Destruction of Bapaume

Bapaume, whose population numbered about 3,000 inhabitants before the war, was systematically and totally destroyed in 1917. Not a house was spared. Those which were not hit by the shells, were either mined or burnt. All the works, factories, sugar-refineries, tanneries and public buildings were ruined. When the British entered the town, the streets were blocked with rubbish of all kinds. Traces of the tar, by means of which the fires had been lit, were still visible on the partially burnt timber-work. Here, as everywhere else, the destructions had been preceded by methodical pillaging.

The bombardments and fighting of 1918 completed the destruction of the town, which, to-day, is entirely in ruins.

ST. NICOLAS CHURCH, BEFORE THE WAR.

BAPAUME.   RUINS OF ST. NICOLAS CHURCH AND BARRACKS.

VISIT TO BAPAUME.

Tourists arriving by the N. 29, enter Bapaume through the suburb of Arras, where, turn to the right.   Cross the railway (l.c.), coming out at the Place Faidherbe, via the Rue d'Arras.

To commemorate General Faidherbe's victory over the Germans near Bapaume on January 3, 1871, a bronze statue was erected in the Place Faidherbe.   This statue was carried off by the Germans, and when the British entered the town in 1917, they found it had mockingly been replaced by an enormous stove-pipe.

In the Place Faidherbe, at the corner of the Rue d'Arras, stood the Hôtel-de-Ville, an interesting building dating from the fifteenth, sixteenth and seventeenth centuries, on the ground-floor of which was a porch formed by a series of arcades.

In 1917, the Germans set fire to it, previous to evacuating the town. On March 25, one week later, a formidable explosion, caused by a bomb with retarded fuse, destroyed all that had been spared by the fire.   Two members of the French Parliament were found dead under the ruins of the building.

Take the Rue de Péronne, on the right of the Place, then the Rue de l'Eglise, on the right, which leads to St. Nicholas Church.

The Church of St. Nicholas was a large fifteenth and sixteenth century pile, with three naves, whose ruins to-day are most impressive.   The belfry has completely disappeared, while all that remains of the body are broken, gaping fragments of the outside walls, a few pillars of the nave and several vaulted bays of the aisles.

Return to the Rue de Péronne, at the end of which are The Promenades. On the right are the ancient ramparts ; a fairly high eminence, near by, was used as an observation-post for the artillery (pretty view over the town).

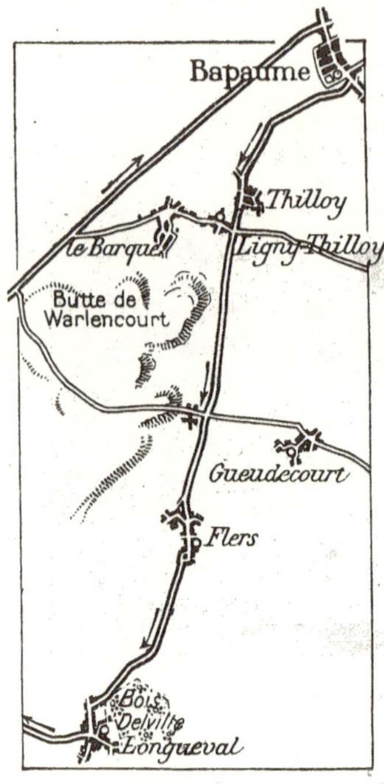

See photo below.

At the end of The Promenades take the G.C. 10, on the right. The road passes through the villages of **Thilloy** and **Ligny-Thilloy**—a single "commune," which likewise includes the village of **Barque.**

It was at and around Ligny-Thilloy that on January 3, 1871, was fought the battle of Bapaume. This unavailing victory of General Faidherbe's forced the Germans to evacuate Bapaume and begin their retreat towards the Somme. In October, 1914, during the fighting which took place near Thilloy, the Germans "compelled a group of some ten women and children to stand before them and face the French positions, then, kneeling behind them, they opened fire on the French troops" (*Report of the Commission of Enquiry*).

In 1917, the fighting in this region was again in favour of the Allies, as on February 27–28, after a feeble resistance, the villages of Barque, Ligny and Thilloy were captured by the British.

The industrial and agricultural "*Commune*" of Ligny-Thilloy, which had already suffered severely during the war of 1871, was completely ruined by the late War.

One kilometre beyond Ligny, there is a mine-crater on the right of the road.

At the crossing with the Gueudecourt road stands a large cross, erected to the memory of the New Zealanders who fell around there. *Keep straight on to* **Flers**—completely ruined. In May, 1919, two damaged tanks were still to be seen at the entrance to the village.

This was one of the villages captured by the British during their offensive of September 15, 1916.

The Report of the Commission of Enquiry contains the following :—

"During the first month of the German occupation, M. Delmotte, baker,

BRITISH CROSS.
See above sketch-map.

RUINS OF FLERS VILLAGE.

was ordered to supply the enemy with bread.   He complied with their demands, without, however, receiving anything in exchange, except requisition forms. Some time afterwards, his stock of flour having run out, he was forced to procure some from Bapaume at his own expense.   The Germans having meanwhile taken possession of the mill, it was they who sold him the flour. Finding this arrangement unsatisfactory, he subsequently refused to work any longer for the German soldiers unless at least the flour which he had to buy were paid for.   The Germans, displeased at this, sought an opportunity to revenge themselves.   On October 14, they ordered Delmotte to hand over his fowling-piece, which he did without protesting.   Two days later they directed him to deliver up his ammunition.   Again complying with their request, he handed over a box containing a few cartridges, shell splinters, and two cartridge

BRITISH TANKS AT ENTRANCE TO FLERS VILLAGE, MAY, 1919.

DELVILLE WOOD.

clips which his son had picked up in the fields. He was immediately arrested
for detaining arms and locked up in his cellar, where he was closely watched.
The next day he was shot in his garden, beside a grave which his murderers
had dug beforehand."

*Beyond Flers, G.C. 197—which forms the continuation of G.C. 10—although
in bad condition, is passable with careful driving.* It crosses a devastated,
shell-torn region, in which are numerous graves, shelters and gun-emplacements.
Before reaching Longueval, it skirts the western edge of **Delville Wood,** the
skeleton remains of which are to be seen on the left.

THE DEVIL'S TRENCH, DELVILLE WOOD.

GERMAN CEMETERY, BETWEEN DELVILLE WOOD AND LONGUEVAL.

Beyond the wood, before entering Longueval, a German cemetery with 200 graves is seen on the left, near the railway (photo above).

Delville Wood and Longueval were the scene of desperate fighting during the latter part of July, 1916.

These two positions had been brilliantly carried by the British on July 14 and 15, in spite of their powerful defences, but German counter-attacks with lachrymatory and asphyxiating gas shells, forced the British to fall back a few days later. However, the latter soon returned to the attack, and a terrible struggle began, which lasted five days and nights without intermission (July 23 to 28).

One South African Brigade gave proof of marvellous courage and endurance in Delville Wood, where, attacked by nine and a half battalions, supported by an overwhelming artillery, it did not yield an inch of ground. One group of machine-gunners was reduced to one man, who continued to fire, until his gun jammed, when he coolly took it to pieces, set it right and resumed firing. Only after he had emptied all his cartridge belts did he withdraw. In another corner of the wood, Scottish units, on the point of being surrounded, charged with bayonet and grenades, and in spite of the enemy's numerical superiority, succeeded in cutting their way through, after a furious hand-to-hand struggle. On July 28, the wood was finally cleared of its last German occupants. On both sides the losses were very heavy. Three German regiments were completely annihilated.

The desperate nature of the struggle is attested by the present aspect of Longueval village and Delville Wood. It is almost impossible, even with the

WHERE LONGUEVAL CHURCH USED TO STAND.

At the back: DELVILLE WOOD.

help of a map, to locate the site of this once pleasant spot amid this chaos of stones and bricks, tree-stumps and shell-torn ground.

In Longueval, take the Contalmaison road, on the right.

Two kilometres beyond Longueval, turn to the left towards **Bazentin-le-Grand.**

Bazentin-le-Grand was a small hamlet, belonging to a large agglomeration of houses (now razed to the ground), of which Bazentin-le-Petit was the continuation.

After capturing Contalmaison and Mametz Wood in July, 1916, the British soon reached and carried Bazentin-le-Grand.

A desperate struggle then began on July 14, 1916, before Bazentin-le-Petit. To the strains of the *Marseillaise* the British attacked the German entrenchments, captured and lost the village several times, and finally remained masters of it. To consolidate the conquered ground they immediately advanced beyond it.

Penetrating into the German third line, they gained a footing in Foureaux Wood (High Wood), and on the slopes of Hill 155.

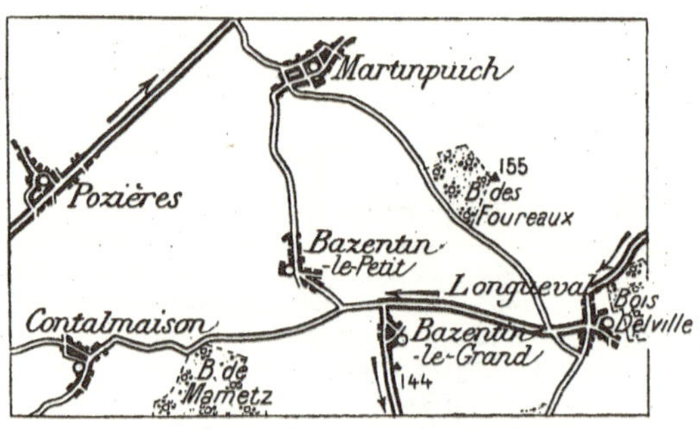

A squadron of British Dragoon Guards—the first appearance of British cavalry in the trench warfare—charged the wood, spreading panic in the enemy ranks.

Foureaux Wood, literally covered with formidable defences, was only captured after two months of incessant fighting. Finally, the last defenders, surrounded on all sides, were forced to surrender on September 15.

In August, 1918, the British, after piercing the lines on the Ancre and Thiepval Plateau, attacked the German forces, not, as in 1916, parallelly to the Albert-Bapaume road, but at right-angles to it. In two days (August 25–26) they captured Contalmaison village, Mametz Wood, Bazentin, Foureaux Wood and Martinpuich, to the east of the road.

Pass through Bazentin-le-Grand. The road crosses Hill **144,** *then descends to a quarry on the left,* in which several hundred British soldiers were buried. *It next climbs up to* **Montauban**—a village rising tier upon tier on the slope of an eminence, the top of which, slightly further to the west (Hill 136), is one of the highest spots in the whole region between Albert and Péronne.

The road passes a cross (photo above) in the village, at the junction of two ways. Take the one on the right, which leads to the site of the late church. Of the latter, nothing remains but a few iron crosses in the surrounding cemetery (*photo below*).

Montauban was captured by the British on the first day of their offensive (July 1, 1916). The struggle was short, but fierce and sanguinary. Numerous machine-guns posted in the cellars of the houses directed a continuous and murderous fire upon the assailants through the vent-holes, and had to be destroyed one by one, by means of grenades. The enemy losses were very heavy. During the artillery preparation, and on the day of the attack, the Bavarian 6th Regiment lost 3,000 men out of 3,500 ; the casualties of another of their Infantry Regiments (the 190th) amounted to half its total strength.

Since the third month of the war, Montauban had remained quite close to the front line, and was reduced to ruins. The few houses spared by the Allies' artillery were destroyed later by the German guns.

It is utterly impossible to locate the site of a street or house. The only remaining landmarks are the pond and the cemetery—the latter considerably enlarged by the addition of numerous German graves. Everywhere else nothing is to be seen, except heaps of stones and rubbish, beams, scrap-iron, and débris of all kinds.

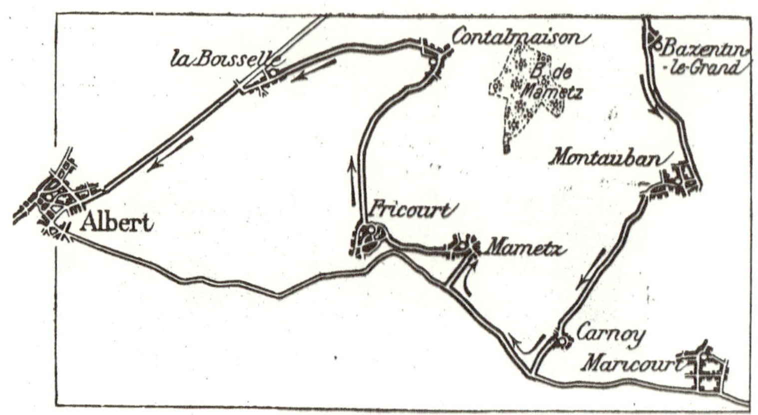

At Montauban Church turn to the right. On leaving the village take the road on the left to **Carnoy.**

It was to the north of Carnoy that from September, 1914, to July, 1916, the front line became fixed.

On July 1, 1916, the British set out from Carnoy to attack Montauban, in *liaison* on their right with the French.

Outside Carnoy the road crosses a ravine, in which runs the short Albert-Péronne railway, and passes a large cemetery on the left. *It next rises sharply to the Albert-Péronne road, which take on the right.*

Two kilometres beyond the fork, take the road to **Mametz,** *on the right.*

The village of Mametz (completely destroyed) was captured by the British on July 1, 1916, in spite of a desperate resistance.

In the village, take the road to **Fricourt** (1 *km.*), *on the left.*

Fricourt village was fortified by the Germans and formed part of their front line until July 1, 1916.

Rising in tiers on the brow of a hill, this village consisted of a continuous series of blockhouses and redoubts, with numerous machine-guns. Underneath the houses were deep, comfortable shelters, some of which were 45 feet deep. As was the case throughout the whole of the sector before Albert,

CONTALMAISON.
SITE OF THE
DESTROYED
CHURCH.

CONTALMAISON.
ENTRANCE TO
THE CHÂTEAU.
*The cellars
were used as
dressing
stations.*

Fricourt was the scene of violent mine warfare for many months. On various occasions sanguinary encounters took place for the possession of the mine-craters, but the front line trenches continued to occupy the same positions. The Germans kept the village, while the French clung to its south-western outskirts.

It took the British no less than thirty-six hours of incessant fighting to carry it on July 2, 1916. 1,500 prisoners were taken.

Take the road to **Contalmaison** (3 *km.*), *which branches off to the right at Fricourt.* Before entering the village notice the British cemetery on the left.

The ancient market-town of Contalmaison was important, on account of its dominating position at the junction of several roads. Surrounded with redoubts and defended by the Prussian Guard, it was taken, then lost, on July 7, 1916. Attacked again from the south and west, it was finally carried on July 11, together with Mametz Wood, lying to the east. Contalmaison was completely destroyed.

A few crosses mark the site of the church and cemetery.

Take the Boisselle road on the left, and return to Amiens, via Albert, a short distance further on.

CONTALMAISON.
BRITISH
CEMETERY
NEAR THE
CHÂTEAU.

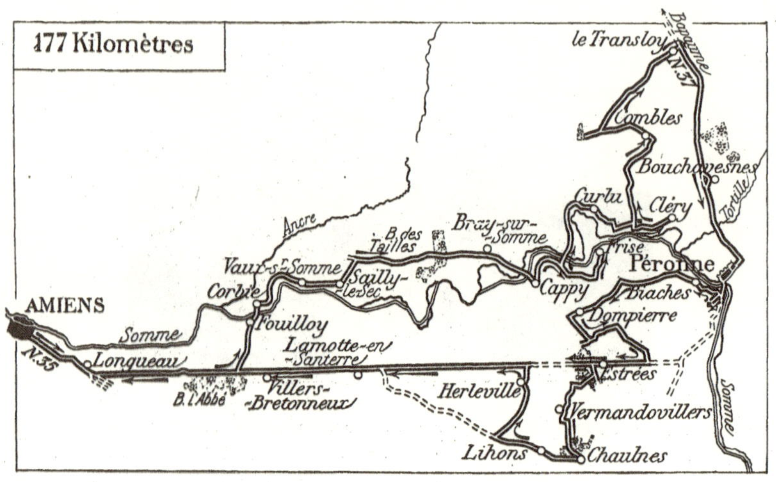

SECOND DAY.

THE VALLEY OF THE SOMME—COMBLES—PÉRONNE.

Leave Amiens by the Rue Jules Barmi (continuation of the Rue de Noyon), then, after passing the station, by the Chaussée Périgord and N. 35.

After passing through Longueau, the road forms a double fork. Take the left-hand road in both cases. At **Petit Blangy** there is an important Australian cemetery on the left. *After twice crossing the railway the road enters* **Abbé Wood.**

On leaving the road, at the foot of a descent (15 km. from Amiens), take the **Corbie** *road on the left, via* **Fouilloy.**

There is a fine 16th–18th century church at Corbie. Restored in the 19th century, it is the remains of a famous abbey. The town suffered severely from the bombardments.

CORBIE.
RUE HERSANT
AND THE
CHURCH.

SAILLY-LE-SEC.

Take the Rue Faidherbe as far as a house with brick turrets, where turn to the right into the Rue Victor Hugo.

Beyond Corbie, the road follows the marshy valley of the Somme to **Vaux-sur-Somme.**

On leaving this village there is a British-American graveyard on the right, by the side of the parish cemetery.

The road next passes through **Sailly-le-Sec,** *whose church is in ruins. At the end of the village take the road on the left, then at the wayside cross, that on the right up Hill 108, past two British cemeteries. 2 km. beyond Sailly-le-Sec, the Corbie-Bray road (G.C. 1) is joined, which take on the right,* past a large British cemetery on the right.

Having crossed **Tailles Wood** *(notice the gun-emplacements) G.C. 1 descends alongside a quarry which sheltered a large German ammunition dump (photo below). 2 km. beyond the quarry, the village of* **Bray-sur-Somme** *is reached.*

NEAR TAILLES WOOD. GERMAN AMMUNITION DUMP.

Bray-sur-Somme

Throughout the offensive of 1916, Bray was an important revictualling centre, and as such, frequently bombed by German aeroplanes. Troops and convoys were constantly passing through.

In 1918, the Germans, having driven back the British beyond the old front line of 1914–1916, occupied Bray on March 26, six days after launching their offensive. Immediately progressing beyond the town, they advanced along the Somme to the vicinity of Sailly-le-Sec, where the front line became fixed at the end of March.

The Franco-British offensive of August 8, the objective of which was to reduce the Amiens Salient, cleared the Somme Valley as far as the outskirts of Bray, where the Germans resisted strongly.

However, on August 22, General Rawlinson's Army, in a fresh effort, succeeded in carrying Hill 107—an observation-post which dominated the country to the north-east. On the night of the 23rd, Australian troops, slipping along the river, entered Bray and captured a large number of prisoners.

The town which, until 1918, had practically escaped damage, suffered severely in the subsequent bombardments, and was moreover thoroughly pillaged by the German troops during their occupation. In this they complied

BRAY-SUR-SOMME. CHURCH AND PLACE DE LA LIBERTÉ.

with the instructions of the High Command, who ordered all the churches and chapels in the region of the Somme to be carefully searched, not excepting the *" altars, confessionals and other parts of the church, access to which is reserved by ecclesiastical rules to the priests only."* In pursuance of this decree, dated May 20, 1918, the church of Bray-sur-Somme was despoiled of its furnishings. A magistrate-member of the Enquiry Commission, visiting the church a few days after the Germans had left, reported : *" A large number of bottles were lying on the floor. The baptismal font was fouled with urine. The door of the Holy of Holies, which bore traces of having been forced, was twisted and the iron-work torn off."*

The church itself (*Hist. Mon.*), dated from the 13th and 15th centuries. It was greatly damaged by the bombardments. The spire collapsed, the façade was pierced with numerous shell-holes, while the timber work and roofing were partly destroyed.

The church is reached by the Rue des Massacres.

After visiting the church, proceed to the bottom of the square, where, on the right, turn to the left into the Rue de Cappy. Pass a Merovingian cemetery, then follow the marshy Valley of the Somme to **Cappy** (*3 km. from Bray*).

CAPPY. THE VILLAGE AND BRIDGE OVER THE CANAL.

Cappy, lost on March 26, 1918, was reconquered exactly five months later by the British. The Germans had a dump in the village for all the sacred articles stolen in the district. This depôt was installed in the yard of the billet occupied by the "*officer in charge of the booty*," opposite a building which, according to a notice posted up by the Germans, was the meeting-place of the "*detachments for the collection of the booty*." The sudden arrival of the British did not leave them time to carry away the booty, which included three bells, a quantity of metallic objects, chandeliers, candlesticks, crucifixes, and "six greatly damaged ecclesiastical ornaments."

The church has a massive fourteenth century fortified belfry, the upper

THE CANAL
NEAR THE LOCK.
WOUNDED ON
THEIR WAY TO
THE DRESSING-
STATION.

story of which comprises four watch-towers resting on the corner abutments. Two of these towers were destroyed by the bombardment.

Near the Church, take the road which runs parallel to the Somme canal. On leaving Cappy there is a large Franco-British cemetery *on the left.*

Eclusier (3 *km. beyond Cappy*) *is next reached ;* it is the principal portion of the " *commune* " of Vaux-Eclusier. **Vaux,** which forms the other portion of it, lies on the northern bank.

On July 1, 1916, the French first lines, passing through the eastern outskirts of Vaux-Eclusier, barred the Valley of the Somme with a continuous line of small posts established in the middle of marshes, thus connecting the organisations on solid ground on the northern bank with those of the southern bank.

There is a French military cemetery on the right, before entering Eclusier.

In spite of numerous bombardments, Eclusier has retained the appearance of a village. Most of the damage is repairable.

It was only in January, 1916, that Vaux-Eclusier became the last village occupied by the French in the Valley of the Somme. Previous to that date the advanced lines ran beyond the village of **Frise,** 2 km. further to the east

FRISE CHURCH IN SEPTEMBER, 1917 (*see pp.* 70–72).

To reach Frise, keep straight along the Somme Canal.

Standing on a picturesque site dominated by a hill on the north, the village lies on the left bank of the Somme, opposite the marshes, at the end of a large bend in the river. This bend measures 7 km. round, whereas the isthmus which separates the two arms of the river, opposite Frise, is scarcely 1 km. in width. These conditions made it very difficult to defend the village,

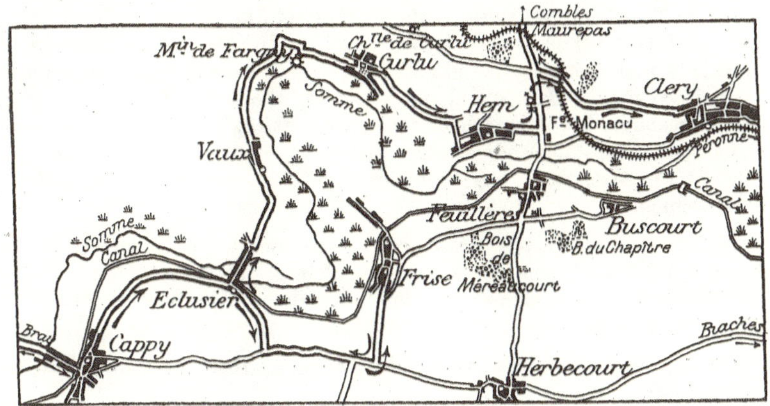

FRISE CHURCH
IN 1919 (*see pp.*
40-42).
*Only the two
trees are left.*

which was accordingly used only as an advance-post. The Germans attempted to capture the place on several occasions by local surprise-attacks and mining. In January, 1916, a powerful attack with large forces succeeded, after a violent bombardment, in occupying the position, but the Germans were unable to debouch from it.

The French retook Frise on the morning of July 2, 1916. In the course of a brilliant attack, the successive lines of trenches which defended the southern and eastern parts of the village, were carried, and the latter was evacuated by the Germans at noon. Giving the enemy no time to reform, the French followed up their success by attacking the German second line, and before nightfall carried that part of Méréaucourt Wood which lies to the east, on a crest about 340 feet high, overlooking the Valley of the Somme.

Frise was completely destroyed. Here and there fragments of walls and half-burnt beams mark the site of the old houses. Some of the inhabitants have returned and are being housed in huts erected in the Place de l'Eglise.

The large modern church has disappeared, the tottering ruins having been pulled down.

VAUX VILLAGE AND THE VALLEY OF THE SOMME.

On leaving Frise, return to Eclusier by the same road. Beyond the church take the road on the right which crosses first the canal, then the marshes by means of three bridges. At the fork, take the right-hand road to **Vaux.**

There is a fine view of the River Somme and the marshes, including part of the battlefield of July 1, 1916. In the valley, walled in by high chalky cliffs, the Somme, bordered with high poplar-trees, follows its winding course among marshes and peat-bogs, intersected with patches of rushes and reed-grass. The half-hidden ruins of Frise are on the right. On the left fragments of walls are all that remain of Fargny Mill and the buildings which surrounded it. The French first line ran close by on July, 1, 1916 (*photo, p.* 74).

FARGNY MILL, JULY, 1916.

Behind, the edge of a once wooded ravine, the chalky substratum of which, laid bare by shell-fire, was christened **"Gendarme's Hat"** by the Poilus, formed the Germans first line.   Further away, in the hollow of the valley, appear the ruins of **Curlu** village.

The road runs alongside the Somme.   At the site of Fargny Mill go round the " Gendarme's Hat "—from which the attack of July 1, 1916, debouched —*to reach* **Curlu.**

Curlu had been transformed into a stronghold by the Germans.

Debouching from Fargny Mill, on the morning of July 1, a regiment of the French 20th Corps carried all the German advance-positions with great dash, notably the " Gendarme's Hat."   However, at the outskirts of Curlu, further advance was stayed by machine-gun fire, making fresh artillery preparation necessary, which destroyed most of the houses.   Rushing again

THE "GENDARME'S HAT," JULY, 1916.

CURLU CHURCH.
Fragment of 13th century wall—all that is left of the village.

to the assault in the evening, the French, in a few minutes, drove the Bavarians from all their positions, and the enemy's numerous attempts during the night and throughout the next day to regain a footing in the village broke down before the French barrage fire.

The day after the capture of Curlu, the French resumed their advance, and soon reached the village of **Hem,** which they carried on July 5, after fierce fighting lasting the whole day.

The road follows the line of the advance, from Fargny Mill to Hem. *At Curlu leave the church on the left.* Numerous shelters, graves and cemeteries are seen along the road, which passes near **Hem-Monacu** (2 *km. beyond Curlu*); a few broken walls, 300 yards to the right of the road, are all that remain of the village (*photo below*).

HEM-MONACU. RUINS OF THE CHURCH.

The French were held to the east of Hem (*see sketch-map, p.* 71), by the strong defences around the village. These positions consisted of: a wood full of barbed-wire entanglements, situated to the north, near the station of the Albert-Péronne light railway; to the north-east, other strongly organised small woods and a quarry.

Further to the east, on the Combles-Feuillères road (G.C. 146), **Monacu Farm**—a veritable fortress with numerous strong-points—was connected with other defences which had been organised in the slag-heaps of the phosphate of lime works belonging to the St. Gobain Glass Manufactory. These defences extended as far as the Somme marshes, where the long reeds hid the numerous machine-guns.

The French carried all these centres of resistance at the end of July and beginning of August, and kept them in spite of fierce German counter-attacks, some of which lasted thirty-six hours. At Monacu Farm the German efforts assumed a particularly violent character. The French artillery, posted on the top of the cliffs, enfiladed the attacking waves, which were each time forced to fall back in disorder with very heavy losses, without being able to reach the French lines.

These successful operations, while enabling the French to secure the whole second line of the German defences, also gave them an outlet, on the north, into Combles Valley—the long, dry and sinuous ravine along which runs the Albert-Péronne light railway. On the south, they also commanded the bridges and roads leading to Feuillères, on the left bank of the Somme.

The bridges were immediately rebuilt, and direct communication ensured between the troops engaged north and south of the river.

Three kilometres from Curlu, take the Feuillères-Maurepas road (G.C. 146) *on the left, to* **Hem Wood** (500 *yards further on*). *Here take the G.C.* 213, *on the right, to* **Cléry-sur-Somme**—an important village on the north of a bend in the river. Fine view of the Somme, towards Péronne.

In the Middle-Ages, Cléry was a fortified town commanding the valley of the Somme. Here the Dukes of Créquy, then lords of the district, built a fortified castle in front of the river marshes, to which the family device: "*Nul s'y frotte*" ("Meddle not with me") was given. Before the war some fourteenth century vestiges of the castle were still to be seen.

CLERY.
CEMETERY
IN
MADAME
WOOD.

In fortifying Cléry, the Germans took full advantage of its favourable position ; powerful defences were made in the outskirts of the village, and in the surrounding woods and ravines, while many of the houses were transformed into centres of resistance. However, in spite of the strength of its defences, Cléry was entirely carried in a single assault on September 3, 1916, after a terrific bombardment which the German *communiqués* qualified as "ferocious."

The success was an important one, as Cléry commanded the various roads leading to Maurepas, Combles and Bouchavesnes on the north, another road on the east leading to Feuillancourt and some bridges across the Somme. The capture of the hamlet of **Omiécourt** at the other end of the bridges, two days after that of Cléry, enabled the French to connect up their positions north of the Somme with those on the left bank of the river. The Germans counter-attacked in force several times, but were unable to retake the position, in spite of very heavy losses.

Cléry was completely destroyed ; only a few broken walls and shattered roofs remain, and even these few traces of the formerly prosperous village are crumbling away and disappearing. A few unrecognisable fragments of ruins, standing amid an accumulation of stones and rubbish, are all that is left of the fifteenth century church.

There are numerous soldiers' graves in the village, and also many military defence-works.

To the east of Cléry the turbid waters of the Somme spread themselves out, forming immense marshes, intersected by a labyrinth-like network of channels. The French advance was directed from this side in 1916, while on the east they were likewise blocked by the Mont-Saint-Quentin Hill, which rises nearly 200 feet above the Somme Valley, from Cléry to Péronne, and which the Germans, by powerful defences, had converted into a second "Warlencourt Ridge." Although within sight of Péronne, scarcely three miles distant, the French could get no farther. Cléry, on the right bank of the Somme, was the nearest village to Péronne conquered by the French in 1916.

MAUREPAS VILLAGE—COMPLETELY RAZED.

In March, 1918, no important engagements were fought on the old Somme battlefields. On March 24 the Germans crossed the Somme, south of Péronne, and forced the Tortille line north of the town. Overwhelmed and in danger of being surrounded, the British had to fall back hurriedly, under the protection of rear-guards, who were unable to check the enemy's advance.

In the following month of August the valley of the Somme was cleared of the enemy almost without firing a shot. In accordance with Marshal Foch's general plan, the British attack of August 21 was limited to the north of the Somme. The Germans had just been driven back, south of the river, from the district of Montdidier to the outskirts of Roye, as a result of the Franco-British offensive of August 8. The Allied plan provided for the withdrawal of the enemy's right wing from the banks of the Ancre to Bapaume, thereby necessitating the immediate evacuation of the whole bend in the Somme by their centre, and this is what actually happened. As soon as Bapaume was invested, the Germans hastily retreated, and whereas, on August 28, the British were still hanging on to the western outskirts of Curlu, on the morning of the 29th they were in Hem, and in the evening of the same day had progressed beyond Cléry.

On leaving Cléry, return by the same road to Hem Wood, where take the Feuillères-Maurepas road (G.C. 146), on the right towards Maurepas. The road runs alongside Hem Wood (cut to pieces), crosses a ravine in which ran the Albert-Péronne railway, and then rises towards a crest from which starts, on the left, a road (500 yards from the fork) leading to **Maurepas** *(completely destroyed).*

The Germans strongly fortified the village of Maurepas which protected Combles from the south-west and formed the junction of six roads coming **from all directions.** It was an agglomeration of large farms, each of which

MAUREPAS
POND.

possessed a meadow surrounded with trees.   These farms had to be carried almost one at a time, and the advance was therefore very slow.

The first assault against the village was launched on August 12 by troops coming from Hardecourt-aux-Bois ; only the southern and western parts of the village—including the fortified cemetery and the church—could be carried.   The northern part fell a few days later.   Finally, on August 24, the last centres of resistance—notably the houses alongside of the roads leading to Combles and to Forest—were captured.

In the village, near a cross, take the road to **Combles**, *on the right, crossing the north-west part of the village.*   The site of the church is on the right, while on the left is a small German redoubt (*photo below*), from which there is a fine view of **Hardecourt-aux-Bois.**

Hardecourt, which cannot be reached by road, stood at the junction-point of the French and British forces during the offensives which aimed at the investment of Combles.   It had been captured in less than three hours by the French on July 8, 1916, together with the eminence which protects it on the north.   A few scattered ruins are all that remain to-day of the village.

The road runs straight from Maurepas to **Combles** (*3 km.*).

MAUREPAS,
GRAVES
AROUND
A GERMAN
REDOUBT.

PANORAMIC VIEW OF COMBLES

A.—*Trônes Wood*; B.—*Guillemont*; C.—*Ruins of Church*; D.—*Entrance to the Underground emplacement*; H.—*Morval*; I.—*Combles*.

Investment and Capture of Combles by the Franco-British Troops in September, 1916

Combles formed the last redoubt in the German defences until September, 1916.

Nature had made the position an exceedingly strong one. Enclosed at the bottom of a small valley and completely surrounded by a girdle of hills, Combles was out of reach of the artillery. For two and a half years the Germans had been fortifying this position, building formidable entrenchments and extensive subterranean defences in and around the village.

The systematic conquest by the Allies during the first half of September, 1916, of the whole region, including the villages of Forest, Maurepas, Guillemont and Ginchy, had brought about the fall of the whole of the defences of the stronghold, on the south and west.

A fresh Franco-British attack was launched on September 25, after a terrific bombardment, with the object of encircling the fortress, by the capture of the strong points which still protected it on the east and north (*see sketch-map, p.* 81).

...D THE SURROUNDING COUNTRY.

...elters ; E.—Combles-Guillemont road ; F.—Bouleaux Wood ; G.—Quarry used as howitzer
...rval road ; J.—Maurepas-Combles road.

On the south-east, the French, starting from their trenches in the old German positions of Le Priez Farm—a powerful redoubt protected by six lines of defences which they had carried by assault on September 14—captured the hamlet of Frégicourt. On the east, they carried Rancourt village, and

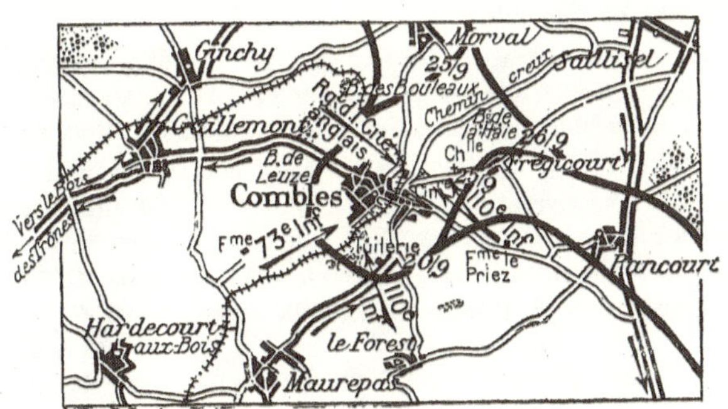

ONE OF THE ENTRANCES TO THE UNDERGROUND
SHELTERS OF LAMOTTE CHÂTEAU.
(*Stretcher-bearers taking a meal.*)

all intermediary positions between these two points, advancing as far as the north-western corner of St. Pierre-Vaast Wood.

On the north, the British took the fortified villages of Morval and Lesbœufs, and nearly joined hands with the French.

The Germans had now only one line of communication with their rear, consisting of a hollow road which, winding towards Sailly-Saillisel to the north-east, through La Haie Wood, was under the fire of the Franco-British artillery. The Germans therefore decided to evacuate their positions, but the Allies did not give them time to withdraw in good order. On the morning of September 26 they attacked again, the objective being this time the defences of the village itself. Their junction was to be the centre of the village and " London " the pass-word. The plan of attack was carried out to the letter. The French 110th Infantry Regiment, debouching from the south-east, carried all that part of Combles lying east and south of the railway, including the cemetery and railway-station. The 73rd Infantry Regiment captured and consolidated the western part of the village, in spite of stubborn resistance. The City of London Regiment cleared the north-western portion of the village.

The streets and the road leading to Sailly-Saillisel, along which the Germans retreated, were filled with their dead ; 1,200 prisoners and important quantities of material and supplies, both food and ammunition, were captured.

Lying partly at the bottom of the valley and rising partly in tiers on the slopes of the surrounding hills, Combles (1,150 inhabitants, mostly engaged in silk and wool weaving) had suffered less from this fierce fighting than might have been expected. Although damaged (shattered walls, disjointed timber-work and tileless roofs) many of its houses were still standing at the end of 1916. The village had, however, been thoroughly pillaged by the Germans, and traces of their long occupation were everywhere to be

IN THE UNDERGROUND SHELTERS OF LAMOTTE CHÂTEAU.
(*German Officers' room.*)

seen, including concrete shelters, strong-points, for machine-guns, underground passages, chambers, etc.

The tunnels, excavated out of the solid rock under the Lamotte Castle, which already existed before the war, were the most important of these subterranean organisations. The Germans utilised them as posts of commandment, dressing-stations, mustering-places, etc. They were large enough to shelter several companies at a time and sufficiently deep to be proof against the heaviest projectiles. There were separate entrances and exits, ventilating shafts, electric light, etc., and they were comfortably fitted up. Beds were installed in the walls, and there were tables, chairs, arm-chairs, tapestries, etc.—all stolen from the houses in the village.

Combles in 1918

In 1918, the British attacked the Combles positions, only after the fall of Bapaume. Gen. Rawlinson's Army remained till August 29, 1918—when Bapaume was taken—on the line reached on the 26th, which ran west of Ginchy, Guillemont and Hardecourt-aux-Bois. Resuming their advance on the 29th and pressing hard upon the heels of the retreating enemy, they carried these three villages the same day, then Maurepas, and finally Combles itself, advancing beyond in the evening.

The ruin of the village was completed during these operations.

Very few houses retained their four walls and roofs. Of the Town Hall a piece of broken wall only remains. The church was almost entirely destroyed, only a few fragments of the façade remain standing amid a heap of stones and rubbish.

On reaching Combles turn to the left and cross the village as far as the ruined church, opposite which is the entrance to the underground passages and chambers of **Lamotte Castle.**

The church stands at the junction of two roads. *Take the right-hand one*

COMBLES CHURCH.
On the right : Guillemont road ; on the left : impassable road to Hardecourt.

(*G.C.* 20) *which rises towards Guillemont village,* built on the top of a hill (altitude 462 feet). The road runs between two small woods—**Bouleaux Wood** (on the right) and **Leuze Wood** (on the left)—both cut to pieces by the shells.

Bouleaux Wood was carried by the British on September 15, 1916. The attack coinciding with a German counter-attack, gave rise to an exceedingly violent encounter. After capturing an important redoubt, east of the wood, the British gradually outflanked the enemy on the wings, and pressing hard from all sides, forcing them to retreat one kilometre northwards at the end of the day.

Leuze Wood was also carried by assault.

The village of **Guillemont** (2 *km. beyond Combles*) *is next reached.*

Guillemont (razed to the ground) was entirely captured by the British on September 3, 1916. No trace whatever remains of the houses, the sites of which are now indistinguishable from the surrounding fields. The whole area was devastated and is now overrun with rank vegetation. After its capture it was strewn with wreckage of all kinds—stones, bricks, beams, agricultural implements, and household furniture from the shattered farms and houses. The fine modern church, Gothic in style, which stood in the centre of the village, has entirely disappeared.

1 *km.* 500 *beyond Guillemont is* **Trônes Wood**, *to reach which, take the Montauban road* (*G.C.* 64) *on the left at the fork of the village.*

GUILLEMONT. SITE OF THE DESTROYED VILLAGE.

MONUMENT TO THE DEAD OF THE BRITISH 18TH DIVISION.

Trônes Wood was the scene of much desperate fighting between the British and the Germans during the first fortnight of July, 1916.

The struggle was almost incessant from July 8 to July 14, the wood changing hands seven times (the Germans say they lost and retook it eighteen times running). On both sides the greatest bravery was displayed, despite terrible losses. British progress was long stayed by a concrete blockhouse (still existent) in the middle of the wood, from which, through slits in the walls, enemy machine-guns rained death unceasingly on the assaulting columns.

A battalion of the Royal West Kents remained forty-eight hours cut off in a corner of the wood to the north-east, and repulsed many furious assaults without loss of ground.

The trees were hacked to pieces by the shells. Among the stumps may be seen trenches, shelters, blockhouses and small forts. In the middle, to the right of the road, is a **pyramid** erected to the memory of the officers and men of the British 18th Division, killed in 1916–1918 in the Battle of the Somme (*photo above*).

At the end of the wood, near a rail track on the right, and fifty yards from the road, is a concrete blockhouse (photo below).

TRÔNES WOOD. MACHINE-GUN BLOCKHOUSE.

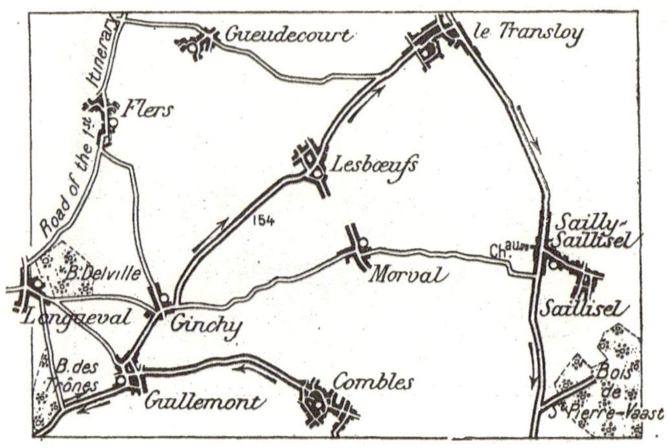

Return by the same road to the fork at Guillemont, and take the road on the left (leaving that going to Combles on the right). 50 yards farther on, take the road to **Ginchy** *on the right.* This little village (1 *km. from Guillemont*) lies on the western slope of the high " Ancien Télégraphe," plateau formerly chosen by Chappe as a telegraph post.

Situated at the crossing of six roads, Ginchy defended Combles (4 km. to the south-east) on the north-west. Partly conquered on September 3, 1916, Ginchy was only completely occupied by the British on September 9, after a terrible struggle lasting three days, in the ruins of the village (entirely destroyed). The Irish troops (Connaught, Leinster and Munster Regiments) particularly distinguished themselves.

Follow the road through Ginchy, leaving on the left the roads to Longueval (passable) and Flers, and, on the right, the road to Morval. There is a British cemetery in Ginchy, on the left. *Keep straight on to Lesbœufs.*

GINCHY. WHERE THE CHURCH USED TO STAND.

LOG ROAD OVER HILL 154.

Beyond Ginchy, the road is made of logs for several kilometres (photo above). It crosses a shell-torn plateau (Hill.154), on which numerous graves convey an idea of the violence of the struggle. In May, 1919, a large German material and ammunition dump, also a rail-track, were still to be seen there.

There is a German cemetery *on the left, this side of Lesbœufs.*

Lesbœufs *village, next reached,* was entirely destroyed ; only a few shell-torn trees and (on the right) a mound of stones and rubbish (the church) remain.

Cross the village and keep straight on to **Le Transloy,** noticing the numerous graves on the right and left.

Of this important village only a few broken walls remain.

After crossing the village N. 37 is picked up ; 100 *yards farther on,* the ruins of a large sugar factory are seen on the left.

Take N. 37 on the right to Péronne, passing through **Sailly-Saillisel,** 4 km. *beyond Transloy.*

LE TRANSLOY. SITE AND RUINS OF CHURCH.

SAILLY-SAILLISEL.
As seen when looking towards Péronne.

The Capture of Sailly-Saillisel by the French

(October—November, 1916.)

Having taken Combles, the French hastened to consolidate their gains by carrying the height of Sailly-Saillisel (in October, 1916)—the last of the hills from which the Germans dominated the hollow of Combles. On this hill (altitude, 455–488 ft.) stood an extensive village formed by two agglomera tions—**Sailly,** grouped around the Bapaume-Péronne road (N. 37) and **Saillisel,** built to the south-east and along G.C. 184.

Daily progress by means of grenade fighting having enabled the French gradually to encircle Sailly-Saillisel from the north-west to south-west during the first half of October, an attack was then launched against the defences proper of the village. This attack developed into one of the hardest and bloodiest battles in the whole of the Somme offensive, which, begun on October 15, lasted till November 11, 1916.

Sailly was captured first (October 15), the French attacking the defences of the castle, park and old church which flanked Sailly on the west. After desperate fighting, the Germans were forced to retreat. Following up their success, the French pursued the retreating enemy into their second lines and entered the village, reducing the fortified houses one by one, and occupying the whole of the village west of the Bapaume-Péronne road. By nightfall, the central cross-roads of Sailly was reached. On the 16th, a new block of houses was carried. On the 17th, the Germans counter-attacked furiously several times in force, and succeeded in regaining a footing in the defences lost the day before, to which they clung desperately. The capture of the village was only completed on the 18th, when the French consolidated their gains by carrying the ridges which dominate Sailly from the west and north.

The honour of taking Sailly fell to the 152nd Infantry Regiment of the

Vosges, already famous by the capture, in Alsace, of the village of Steinbach and the Hartmannsweillerkopf. For eight days, this gallant unit "*fully maintained its gains, in spite of the most intense bombardment, and as many as three violent counter-attacks daily*" (Order of the Day of December 4, 1916, being the third Citation " à l'ordre de l'Armée " of this regiment).

The battle was soon resumed with the same violence for the possession of Saillisel. At the end of October, the French reached the church—about 200 yards from the first houses of the hamlet—and continued to advance on the following days, occupying Saillisel almost entirely on November 5.

They were, however, unable to maintain themselves there, and the Germans, after extremely violent fighting, reoccupied the ruins of the hamlet. Saillisel was finally and totally conquered on November 11–12. A party of German machine-gunners in a block of houses refused to surrender, and had to be overpowered with bombs.

Sailly-Saillisel must be added to the long list of the villages which have totally vanished. The old castle is now a shapeless mass of ruins. The park was so badly cut up by the shells that there remain practically no vestiges of the trenches and fortifications which the Germans had accumulated there. All the trees were more or less shattered, and rank vegetation now overruns the whole place. Groups of graves scattered here and there, recall the terrible battles which were fought there.

Of the church, only the bases of a few pillars remain. The graves in the churchyard were torn open by the bombardments, and the village was almost entirely levelled.

To visit Saillisel, take, opposite a large pool, a road—at right angles to N. 37— which runs past the ruins of the church : follow it as far as the cross-roads. The sight is impressive, on account of the large number of French graves and shell-holes ; some of the latter are of enormous size.

Return to and follow N. 37 to **Rancourt** *(3 km.). The road crosses Hill* 148, whence there is an extensive view, which explains why the Germans clung so stubbornly to this ground.

On the left of the road, at this point, lies St.-Pierre-Vaast Wood, a visit to which is both impressive and interesting. Access to it is gained by a road which branches off N. 37 at the entrance to Rancourt (see sketch-map, p. 90).

St. Pierre-Vaast Wood

St. Pierre-Vaast Wood, of which nothing remains but shattered, burnt tree-stumps, was the most important vestige of the immense Arrouaise Forest that covered the whole of this region in the Middle-Ages.

From November, 1916, till March, 1917, this wood was often mentioned in the French and, later, in the British communiqués. The Germans had powerfully entrenched themselves there, and it was here that they had their reserves and artillery. In the thickets was a maze of trenches and fortified redoubts, surrounded by minor defence-works of all kinds.

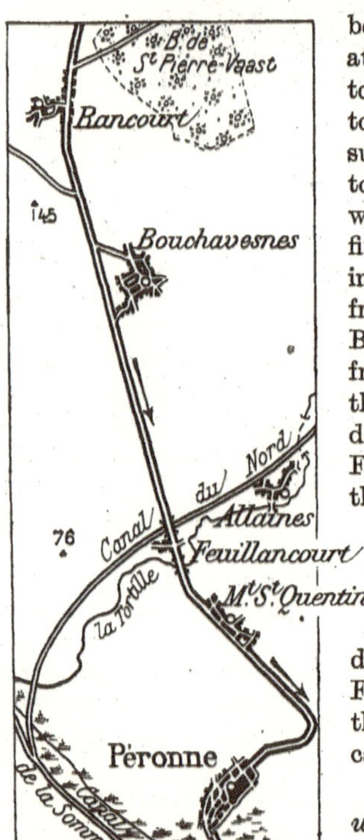

The French partly occupied the wood at the beginning of November, but violent counter-attacks by three enemy army corps forced them to evacuate the conquered ground. Driven back to the western edge of the wood, they were subsequently unable, in spite of renewed efforts, to get beyond it. Throughout the whole winter of 1916–17, the front line remained fixed in front of this wood, which, transformed into an immense stronghold, protected Péronne from the north. This sector, occupied by the British, was never quiet. Grenade fighting from trench to trench was incessant, whilst the artillery gradually annihilated all the defences and levelled the wood almost entirely. Finally, on March 16, 1917, at the beginning of the German retreat on the Somme, the British captured the whole wood, without encountering serious resistance.

After visiting the wood, return to N. 37, and go on to **Rancourt.** This village (entirely destroyed, *photo, p.* 91) was carried by the French on September 25, 1916, in the course of their turning movement which preceded the capture of Combles.

On leaving Rancourt, N. 37 crosses Hill 145, where, on the right, the Combles—Guillemont —Montauban—Albert road begins (passable). This area is thickly strewn with graves.

N. 37 next descends to the beginning of the road to **Bouchavesnes,** *the site of which is seen* 300 *yards to the left.*

The conquest of Bouchavesnes was a stirring episode in the battle of the Somme.

On September 12, 1916, a French detachment, composed of Alpine Chasseurs and infantry, carried the position within two hours, after an intense artillery preparation. In spite of a most stubborn resistance, all the entrenchments and strong points among the ruins of the houses were carried one after the other, in a single rush. 400 men, the only survivors of the two German

RANCOURT

battalions which held the village, were taken prisoners; 10 guns and 40 machine-guns were likewise captured.

The success was so complete and crushing that for a short time there was a gap in the German front line. Scattered units hastily got together were thrown into the breach where, crouching in the shell-holes, they resisted desperately with rifle and machine-gun, and held their ground for a whole day, without any reserve support.

On March 24, 1918, the German columns forced the line of the Tortille stream and entered Bouchavesnes, thereby bringing about the fall of Péronne —outflanked from the north—and the retreat of the British towards the Ancre. The village was reconquered on September 1 following, after sharp fighting.

After passing by Bouchavesnes, N. 37 ascends another crest (see fortified quarry on the left), from the top of which there is a magnificent panorama: *on the left*, the Valley of the Tortille (a small tributary of the Somme); *in the valley*, the Northern Canal and Village of Allaines; *opposite*, the Mont-St.-Quentin; *on the right*, the Valley of the Somme.

The portion of the National road which is now followed was the scene of furious, bloody fighting in 1916. In their attempt to outflank Péronne, the French encountered strong German forces which stubbornly held their ground. Traces of the desperate fighting are seen all along the way: stumps of shattered trees, mine-craters and shell-holes in the fields, soldiers' graves, etc.

BOUCHA-
VESNES.

NEAR PÉRONNE.   RUINS OF BRIDGE OVER THE CANAL DU NORD, ON THE N. 37

Cross the Northern Canal by temporary bridge.
This canal, which connects the Somme with the rivers of northern France, was not quite finished when the war broke out.   Its bed was excavated, but

THE CANAL DU NORD FORMED A BITTERLY DISPUTED LINE
OF RESISTANCE,

WHAT THE GERMANS SAW FROM THEIR OBSERVATION-POST ON THE
MONT-ST.-QUENTIN.

not yet filled with water, so that it formed a ready-made line of resistance.
The Germans were unable to hold it in 1916, and the British were likewise
driven from it by the German thrust in 1918.

Immediately beyond the canal, the small, ruined village of **Feuillancourt** *is
crossed.* On September 12, 1916, the French gained a footing on Hill 76,
west of the village. This was the nearest position to Péronne reached in 1916,
to the north of the town.

Follow N. 37 to **Mont-St.-Quentin.**

Mont-Saint-Quentin

Built along the National road, 2 km. north of Péronne, on a hill having
an altitude of 325–390 ft., the village of Mont-St.-Quentin possessed, until
the Revolution, an important abbey, which was founded in the early Middle
Ages.

The hill, now famous, rises in front of Péronne, and forms the immediate
defence of the town. The Germans had, prior to the Franco-British offensive
of 1916, posted their heavy artillery there and built powerful entrenchments.

From 1914 to 1917 the German pioneers consolidated the position.
The hill was pierced from all sides by subterranean timber-propped galleries,
some leading to immense and comfortable shelters, others to numerous
invisible observation-posts, so placed as to command an extensive view in
all directions.

A large number of camouflaged heavy guns were posted on the slopes of
the hill, the neighbouring observation-posts ensuring great accuracy of fire.

Trenches had been dug all about, in the chalky soil. At the foot of the
slopes, two first-lines completely surrounded the hill, and two similar lines
ran round half-way up. Communication-trenches zig-zagged transversely,

GERMAN OBSERVATION-POST ON MONT-ST.-QUENTIN (IN THE CHÂTEAU PARK).
Péronne and Maisonnette Hill are in the background.

connecting the various lines of main trenches, while the intervening empty spaces were covered with deep entanglements of barbed wire and *chevaux-de-frise*. Lines of barbed wire protected the winding communicating trenches. At the corners, at regular intervals, concrete observation and special posts, all strongly fortified, were built for the machine-gunners and sharp-shooters.

The village itself was powerfully fortified. An intricate system of trenches entirely covered the place, the castle forming the main strong-point. A maze of communication trenches and entrenchments ran throughout the park. A concrete observation-post on the terrace, near the enclosing wall, hidden among the lime-trees, commanded a view of the whole battlefield

SPY-HOLE OF THE OBSERVATION-POST.

MONT-ST.-QUENTIN. RUINED HOUSES.

north and south of the Valley of the Somme.   A subterranean shelter beneath this observation-post connected the defences of the castle with those in the cellars of the village houses.

These powerful entrenchments have almost completely disappeared. Before evacuating the position in March, 1917, the Germans mined the defence-works of the hill, blocking up the entrance to the underground passages. They also set fire to the timber props which supported the roof and walls of the galleries and shelters ; an immense fire was thus lighted inside the hill, which, for several days, had the appearance of a volcano in eruption.

Whilst in 1917 the Germans voluntarily evacuated Mont-Saint-Quentin, they were driven from it by main force in 1918.   During the night of August 30, Australian units, slipping through the brushwood and barbed-wire entangle-ments which covered the steep slopes of the hill, succeeded in reaching the top, and quickly bombed the surprised garrison into submission, about a

MONT-ST.-QUENTIN. GERMAN DEFENCES.

MONT-ST.-QUENTIN. VILLAGE IN RUINS.

third of the defenders being taken prisoners. In spite of fierce counter-attacks, the Australians held their ground the next day. Several assaulting waves, composed of soldiers from the Prussian Guard, were successively launched against the hurriedly consolidated positions, but were each time mowed down by artillery barrages.

Of the village of Mont-Saint-Quentin, nothing remains but the basements of the houses, with here and there bits of broken walls, tottering beams and heaps of rubbish. The church, a favourite pilgrimage, in memory of the former abbey, was totally destroyed, as was also the castle.

The ruins of the castle, and a German observation-post of concrete, with underground passages and shelters, are at the entrance to the village, on the left, about 50 yards from N. 37.

There is a fine panoramic view over the Somme Valley and Péronne.

On leaving Mont-Saint-Quentin, N. 37 descends to **Péronne.** *Enter the town by the Faubourg de Bretagne.*

MONT-ST.-QUENTIN. RUINS OF THE CHÂTEAU.

PÉRONNE.

Péronne, a sub-prefecture of the " Départemont " of the Somme, was one of the centres of the sugar and hosiery industries in France, with a pre-war population of about 5,000 inhabitants.

Built at the junction of the Rivers Somme and Cologne, which form a picturesque girdle of marshes and ponds before the walls of the town, Péronne was formerly a fortified city. Its brick ramparts and moats were being dismantled when the late war broke out.

Origin and Chief Historical Events

Péronne, whose origin goes back to a Merovingian villa built there in the seventh century, became, in the Middle-Ages, an important fortified city, under the rule of the Counts de Vermandois. One of them kept Charles-le-Simple imprisoned there until his death (929). Philippe I. annexed Péronne to the Crown lands, but in 1435 Charles VII. gave the city to Philippe-le-Bon, Duke of Burgundy. In 1483, during the rebellion of the Liégois, Louis XI., who was then the guest of Charles-le-Téméraire, was kept a prisoner in the castle and compelled to sign a humiliating treaty—called the Péronne Peace —which he afterwards refused to fulfil.

In 1536, the Spaniards, under the leadership of the Prince of Orange, besieged the town for thirty consecutive days, but thanks to the bravery of the inhabitants, and the heroism of a woman named Catherine de Poix, or Marie Fouché, who was the soul of the resistance (*photo, p.* 104), Péronne was saved.

The " Holy League," which marked the commencement of the Religious Wars, was founded at Péronne in 1577 by the nobility and clergy.

In 1870–71, the Germans besieged the town for thirteen days (December 28 to January 9), and subjected it to a violent bombardment, which caused considerable damage, though insignificant in comparison with the depredations of the late war. The church, especially the belfry, was greatly damaged, part of it collapsing, and a number of houses were either burnt or destroyed. During the occupation the enemy committed no excesses.

Péronne—whose arms bear the following device, "Urbs nescia vinci" (the undefeated city)—was decorated in 1913 for its gallant conduct in 1536 and 1870–1871.

Péronne during the Great War

In 1914, during their rapid advance on Paris, the Germans entered Péronne (August 28), but were driven out on September 15. They reoccupied the town ten days later (September 24), and remained there until March 17, 1917. A year later (March 25, 1918) the British were compelled to evacuate the town, outflanked as they were from the north and south by the ever-increasing numbers of the German columns marching on Amiens. They re-entered the town on September 1, after a series of very fierce engagements which lasted the whole day.

SAFE DYNAMITED BY THE GERMANS.

Péronne was totally destroyed, partly by the Franco - British artillery, but especially by the systematic destructions on the part of the Germans.

Before retreating in 1917, the Germans set fire to or blew up a large number of houses. Special detachments in charge of the destructions made large rents in the masonry-work, before firing the mines, to ensure total destruction.

The fighting in 1918 completed the ruin of the city, which will have to be entirely rebuilt. A few name-plates on the broken walls, and broken shop-signs alone made it possible to identify the heaps of ruins which lined the streets.

The streets leading from the castle to the southern part of Péronne, and thence to the suburb of Paris (completely ruined), were devastated. The long Rue Saint-Fursy, especially, was almost entirely destroyed.

To the east of the town, the railway-station—connected with Péronne by an embankment across the marshes of the Somme—has retained a portion of its shell-torn frame-work, but the bridges across the marshes, as well as the railway-bridge, were broken.

The cemetery (*about* 1 *km.* 800 *beyond the town*) was devastated. Many graves were desecrated, and trenches dug among the violated sepulchres. A battery of artillery was even posted on the site of ancient vaults. These profanations did not prevent the Germans from burying their dead in a corner of the cemetery, or erecting funeral monuments to their memory.

PÉRONNE. TRENCH IN CEMETERY.

Everywhere pillage preceded destruction. The houses, whose walls (more or less damaged) still remain standing, were completely emptied. The doors, partition-walls, windows and wood-work were taken out and burnt. All the safes, including those of the Banque de France, were broken open. All articles of any value were carried away, and the rest destroyed. In 1917, mattresses ripped open, battered perambulators and cradles, broken furniture, dislocated pianos, even books and family photographs, torn to pieces, were found among the ruins. In the gardens, the fruit-trees were either cut down or hacked at their roots.

PÉRONNE IN 1918. THE GRANDE PLACE. CAPTURED GERMAN GUNS.

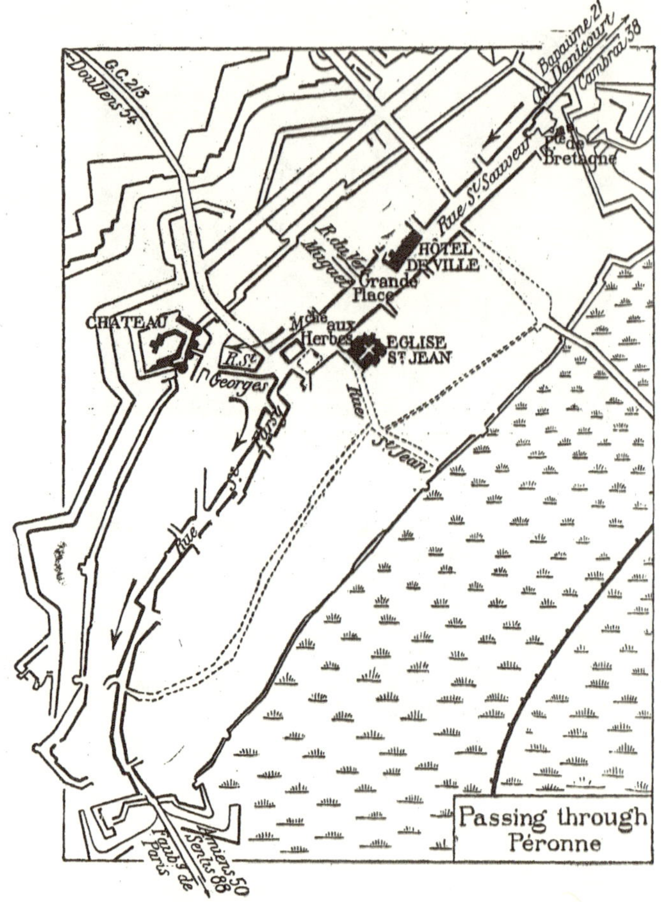

VISIT TO PÉRONNE.

On reaching the town by N. 37, cross the Faubourg de Bretagne, the roadway of which was, in places, destroyed by mines. In 1917 this suburb had suffered less than the other parts of the town. Many of the houses could easily have been repaired, had they not sustained in 1918 new and much more important damage.

At the end of the suburb stands the Bretagne Gate, built of brick and stone. This interesting specimen of late sixteenth century military architecture—although the vaulting bears the date of 1602—is preceded by another eighteenth century gate, and surrounded by remains of the old fortifications. Although struck by shells several times, and rather severely damaged, its vital structure is still standing (*photos, p.* 101).

Follow the Avenue Danicourt, which leads to the Rue Saint-Sauveur.

BRETAGNE GATE. EXTERIOR FAÇADE.

The Rue Saint-Sauveur and the Grande Place which prolongs it, formed the centre of the town, and there the finest shops were to be found. This part of the town was the most completely destroyed of all.

Some half-burnt, dilapidated house-fronts without roofs are still standing ; the other buildings were destroyed by fire or explosions. The adjacent streets are in the same pitiable condition.

BRETAGNE GATE. INTERIOR FAÇADE.

The Grande Place and Hôtel-de-Ville

The Hôtel-de-Ville, in which the Museum was installed, was built in the sixteenth century, but was restored and enlarged in the eighteenth century.

Of its Renaissance west front, facing the Grande Place, only the lower part—in ruins—remains, forming a porch with balcony (*photos, p. 103*)

The carved salamanders which ornamented it were smashed with blows from hammers.

Two of the arcades of the porch collapsed in 1918 (*see second photo on p. 103*).

The Louis XVI. south front, facing the Rue Saint-Sauveur, was less damaged (*photo below*).

The roof and the modern belfry which surmounted the building were

PÉRONNE.   THE HÔTEL-DE-VILLE.
The front facing the Rue Saint-Sauveur.

blown up in 1917.   An unexploded bomb with connecting wires was found in the broken frame-work, fixed to a beam.   Before evacuating the town, the Germans fixed a large wooden board on the west front, bearing the following inscription : *Nicht ärger, nur wundern* (Don't be angry, only admire).

The roof fell in, breaking the ceiling of the rooms in which the Museum and Library were installed.   Some statues were decapitated, and other works of art mutilated.   Books, manuscripts, documents and municipal records were destroyed by the rain which fell through the gaping ceilings.

However, the most valuable works in the Museum were saved, as they had been carried off to Germany.   A few famous paintings may be mentioned, including, "*The Attack of the Railway Station at Strying*," an episode in the battle of Forbach (Alphonse Neuville), another by the same artist, "*Hunting in St. Pierre-Vaast Wood*," in which De Neuville is shown sur-

PÉRONNE.   THE HÔTEL-DE-VILLE BEFORE THE WAR.
*The Renaissance Façade overlooking the Grande Place, and modern
Belfry.   On the right : The Rue Saint-Sauveur.*

rounded by the notables of Péronne ; and a painting attributed to Breughel
Junior, representing a *Conference at the house of an attorney, at Cambrai ;*
objects connected with the local history, an important collection of numis-
matics, and Gallic, Gallo-Roman and Merovingian antiquities were among
the collection.

Before the war an old fifteenth century house with statues stood in the
Grande Place, at the corner of the Rue du Vert Muguet, near the Hôtel-de-
Ville.

In the Place du Marché-aux-Herbes which adjoins the Grande Place
stood a statue of Catherine de Poix, known as Marie Fouché, the heroine of
the siege of 1536.   This statue—like that of General Faidherbe at Bapaume—
was stolen by the Germans during the first occupation of the town.   When

PÉRONNE.   THE HÔTEL-DE-VILLE IN 1917.
*Note the German inscription on the ruined building which the enemy
had deliberately blown up.   (See text.)*

PÉRONNE.   THE PLACE DU MARCHÉ-AUX-HERBES BEFORE THE WAR.

In the background, on the right: Rue St. Fursy and the old house seen in the photograph on p. 75.   In the background: Statue of Catherine de Poix, heroine of the Siege of 1536.

the 1st Warwickshire Regiment entered Péronne on March 17, 1917, they found a grotesque dummy figure on the pedestal *(photo, p.* 105).

At the end of the Place, near the entrance to the Rue St. Fursy, a late fifteenth century wood-panelled house *(photo, p.* 105), ornamented with curious statues of saints and bishops, was burnt down.

THE PLACE DU MARCHÉ-AUX-HERBES IN 1919.

In the foreground: Pedestal of Statue (see above) carried off by the Germans.

PÉRONNE. THE PLACE DU MARCHÉ-AUX-HERBES BEFORE THE WAR.
Seen from the Rue St. Fursy. The 15th Century wooden house on the right, in the foreground, was burnt down. In the background: Church of St. Jean.

There is a fine charcoal drawing of it by Alphonse de Neuville in the Museum.

On the other side of the Grande Place, at the entrance to the Rue St. Jean, stands the **St. Jean Church** (*Hist. Mon.*), in fifteenth century flamboyant style, with three naves terminated by a rectangular apse, to-day in ruins.

The Church of St. Jean

Of the St. Jean Church only the gaping, crumbling walls of the main front remain. The northern front collapsed entirely.

PEDESTAL OF THE STOLEN STATUE OF CATHERINE
DE POIX (*see p.* 104).
On the left: Part of the ruins of the St. Jean Church.

PÉRONNE. THE FAÇADE OF ST. JEAN
CHURCH, BEFORE THE WAR.

The sixteenth century square tower, flanked by a round turret (*photo above*) has vanished.

The western portal with its three doors, decorated with fine fifteenth century carvings, was greatly mutilated (*photo below*).

The roof, frame-work, and interior vaulting, which was ornamented with very fine pendentives, collapsed.

Some of the pillars fell down, and most of the dislocated arches have gradually crumbled away under the action of the weather.

The grand organ was greatly damaged ; all the pipes were removed and sent

THE FAÇADE OF ST. JEAN CHURCH IN 1919.

PÉRONNE.   THE PLACE DU MARCHÉ-AUX-HERBES, AND THE RUE ST. GEORGES.
In the background : One of the towers of the Château (see below.)

to Germany.   On the other hand, the seventeenth century, multi-coloured marble reredos of the high and Virgin altars were not severely damaged.

The Rue Saint-Georges, at the south-west end of the Place, leads to the Château.

The four large sandstone towers with conical roofs, which faced the town, used to form part of the *enceinte* of Péronne.

One of the towers was destroyed ; the other three are still standing, although in a greatly damaged condition.

The pointed door between the middle towers was mutilated.

PÉRONNE.   THE FAÇADE OF THE CHÂTEAU AT THE END
OF THE WAR.

THE DESTROYED BRIDGE ON THE OLD RAMPARTS.
On the right is the end of the Rue St. Fursy.

The other parts of the castle, posterior to the Middle-Ages, were either burnt or destroyed by explosions.

Return to the Place du Marché aux Herbes and take on the right the Rue St.

THE OLD RAMPARTS IN THE FAUBOURG DE PARIS.
In the foreground : The destroyed bridge ; In the background : The temporary bridge : On the right : The N. 17 going towards Villers-Carbonnel.

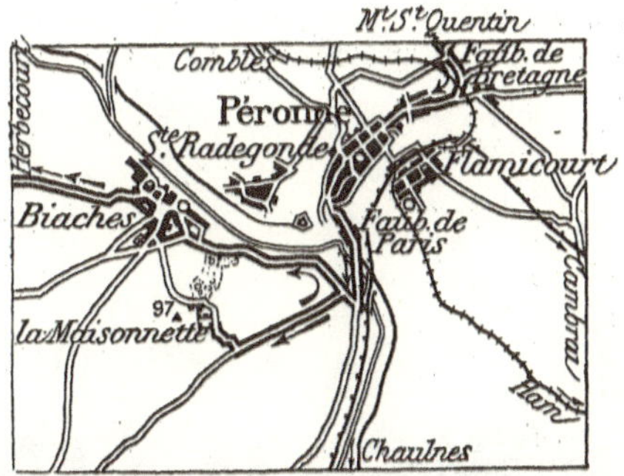

Fursy, which, after crossing the bridges over the old ramparts, leads to the Faubourg de Paris.

At the end of the Faubourg de Paris, take the road to Biaches (G.C. 1) on the right of N. 17; then, 100 yards from N. 17, on the left, the G.C. 79, which climbs the slopes of a hill dominating the valley.

Follow this road for about 1 km., when the top will be reached, from which there is a fine panoramic view of the valley of the Somme, Péronne and Mont-Saint-Quentin *(photo, pp. 110-111).*

Take on foot the path which starts from there, and leads to the ruins of La Maisonnette Château, *about 250 yards from the road.*

La Maisonnette

The estate of La Maisonnette occupied the summit of a limestone eminence which dominates the battlefield south of the Somme (highest point, 320 feet).

In 1870, the German batteries shelled Péronne from this hill. In 1916,

THE BATTLEFIELD AT LA MAISONNETTE.

THE VALLEY OF THE SOMME. PÉRONNE AN

they were determined to hold it at all costs, knowing by experience that the town would soon be untenable with French artillery posted there.

The fighting which took place for the possession of La Maisonnette was of the bloodiest, and made the ruins of the place famous.

The estate comprised a modern château and a park, a second residence close by, about a dozen houses in the vicinity, and some fine trees and orchards. All the houses, thickets and woods—including Blaise Wood, to the north— had been strongly fortified. A maze of entrenchments covered the whole park. A second continuous line of trenches ran round the castle. Loop-holes had been made in the ivy-covered walls of the château. At the corners, and at intervals, in the foundations of the castle, machine-guns were posted. The out-buildings of the estate were similarly fortified. The cellars, some 50 feet deep, were turned into armoured shelters, capable of successfully withstanding the most violent bombardments, and connected with one another and with the defence-works of Blaise Wood by a subterranean passage, which enabled the Germans either to fall back unseen towards the canal or approach for counter-attacks.

However, this did not prevent a French Colonial Regiment from carrying the whole position in an hour and a half on July 9. The cellars were cleared

-ST.-QUENTIN SEEN FROM LA MAISONNETTE.

out with grenades, and the Germans, unable to withstand the impetuous charge of the " Marsouins," surrendered in large numbers. The fiercest fighting took place at Blaise Wood, the defence works of which connected La Maisonnette with Biaches. At this point a German detachment in serried ranks raised their rifles in sign of surrender. As the French advanced to disarm them, the German ranks opened, a hidden machine-gun fired on the French, killing two officers and about fifty soldiers. The French retired, but the lost ground was won back the same day.

On July 15, the Germans counter-attacked furiously, and attempted by means of liquid fire and asphyxiating grenades to slip into La Maisonnette through Blaise Wood. They succeeded in gaining a footing in the northern part of the wood, but were driven out the next day.

On the 17th, six successive assaults were made by the enemy on La Maisonnette hill, but each time the Germans were repulsed with sanguinary losses.

Renewing their attacks, they finally succeeded, first, in gaining a footing in the outskirts of Blaise Wood, and, later, with the help of liquid fire, in penetrating further into the French first lines, where they established themselves in the ruins of the farm.

But, in spite of all their efforts, they were unable to establish themselves securely on Hill 97, to the west of the estate, which dominates the whole valley of the Somme, before and beyond Péronne.

Throughout the winter of 1916–17 constant bombardments, grenade fighting from trench to trench, local attacks with alternating success and failure, made the position on the crest untenable to both sides. Finally, on March 17, 1917, Maisonnette Hill was entirely captured by the Allies, and the Germans fell back on the Hindenburg line, abandoning without striking a blow the few trenches which they had managed to keep on the left bank of the Somme and which they had until then so fiercely defended.

The British, who, early in 1917, had taken over this sector from the French, entered the village, now completely destroyed. The pretty Maisonnette Château had been reduced to a shapeless mass of ruins, while the beautiful park in which it stood was so devastated as to be unrecognisable. The orchards were destroyed, the woods hacked to pieces by shell-fire. Only a portion of the organisations which surrounded the Maisonnette position, and those which connected the hill with Biaches, had withstood the bombardments.

The picture of desolation which met the British soldiers' eyes from the top of Hill 97 was such as no cataclysm could have caused. Nothing was to be seen but devastated lands, destroyed villages and felled trees, while beyond the inundations which had been spread over the Somme marshes, the smoke could be seen rising from the ruins of Péronne, set on fire by the Germans.

Return by the same road to G.C. 1, which take on the left. Follow the Somme for a short distance to the ruins of **Biaches.** This small village formerly nestled in the bottom of a verdant nook near the Canal of the Somme, less than 1 km. from the ancient ramparts of Péronne, and separated from it only by the marshes and the wide and sinuous river.

BIACHES CHURCH AS THE WAR LEFT IT.

In the background : The Marshes of the Somme ; On the right, behind the trees : The beginning of Péronne.

BIACHES.   THE SUGAR REFINERY IN 1916.

The Fighting at Biaches

The fighting at Biaches, like that at La Maisonnette, gave rise to some of the most famous episodes in the Offensive south of the Somme.

The French advance had been so rapid that as early as July 8 General Fayolle's troops, having broken through the German front to a depth of 8 kilometres, occupied the outskirts of Biaches. The next day, after an intense bombardment, the system of trenches which protected the outskirts of the village was carried in a few minutes.

BIACHES.   THE SUGAR REFINERY IN 1919.
Seen from the same view-point.

A desperate struggle which lasted all day took place in the village, where every street and crossing was protected by defence-works. Machine-guns were posted in all the houses, while buildings like the town-hall, sugar refinery, railway-station, etc., had been turned into powerful centres of resistance.

A block of houses to the south-east resisted till the evening, when it was reduced. At the entrance to the village, close to the Herbécourt road, a strong point, passed in the course of the advance, was still in enemy hands.

This position, which subsequently acquired fame under the official name of Herbécourt Redoubt, enabled its occupants to take the French in the rear, and rendered the occupation of the village very difficult and uncertain.

It was absolutely necessary to carry it. Frontal attacks were stopped short by a murderous machine-gun fire ; a concentration of fire with trench-mortars gave no better results. Finally, in the afternoon of July 10, a captain

BIACHES. DEFENCE-WORKS IN THE PLACE DE LA MAIRIE (1916).

and eight men, with " extraordinary daring," crept up to and entered the redoubt. The garrison, which still numbered 112 men and 2 officers, lost their presence of mind and surrendered without offering any resistance.

The loss of Biaches, which formed the last advanced defences of Péronne, was a particularly hard blow for the Germans, who attempted, on several occasions to reconquer the position by fierce counter-attacks.

On July 15, a terrific bombardment was opened on the village. The ruined houses collapsed, fires broke out, and most of the shelters, including those under the cellars, were smashed in. The attack followed in the evening. Leaving Péronne by the Faubourg de Paris, the Germans, favoured by fog, slipped along the banks of the canal and reached the French first lines, which they attacked with liquid fire.

One section, surrounded with flames, gave way. Taking advantage of this, the enemy slipped into the village and, after a violent engagement, conquered the greater part of it, only to be driven out again the next day by a counter-attack, during which the French won back all the lost ground.

BIACHES. THE PLACE DE LA MAIRIE IN 1916.

In the evening of July 17, the enemy made another powerful effort. Supported by heavy batteries posted above Péronne on Mont-Saint-Quentin Hill, which kept up an uninterrupted fire, the Germans again entered Biaches and captured it. The struggle continued throughout the next day in the ruins of the village with varying fortune, and it was only on the 19th that the enemy were definitely driven out.

Further counter-attacks were launched afterwards, but met with no better success. From July 17, 1916, till March, 1917, the French and, later, the British maintained their lines intact in front of Péronne, on the edge of the Somme Marshes.

On leaving Biaches, G.C. 1 rises towards Herbécourt. Looking back, there is a very fine view of Biaches, Péronne and the valley (*Panorama, pp. 116–117*).

3 km. 500 beyond Biaches, leave, on the left, the village of **Flaucourt** (completely destroyed), which was carried by storm on July 3, 1916. **Herbécourt** *is 1 km. 500 farther on.*

BIACHES. THE PLACE DE LA MAIRIE IN 1919.

PANORAMA OF BIACHES
as seen from the Biacl.es

At the entrance to the village, on the left, is a large German cemetery, and on the right a house (almost intact) in which a German dressing-station was installed. German frescoes may still be seen on the walls (*photo, p.* 117).

After capturing Dompierre on July 1, 1916, the French advanced so rapidly on Herbécourt that the Germans were unable to make use of the numerous defence-works which had been accumulated between the two villages. The

TRENCH ON THE HERBÉCOURT PLATEAU.

AND PÉRONNE,
Herbécourt road.

hill overlooking Herbécourt was carried in a few minutes, and on July 2, the village itself was entirely conquered.

The French had thus advanced about 4 km. in depth, and the German second

HERBÉCOURT. HOUSE, PRACTICALLY UNDAMAGED, DECORATED BY THE GERMANS WITH FRESCOES.
It was used as a dressing-station.

HERBÉCOURT. RUINS OF THE CHURCH.

line of resistance was broken into in front of Péronne (6 km. to the east), *i.e.*, at its weakest point.

Herbécourt commands a crossing of roads which branch off in various directions. Rapid communication with the south of the plateau was now possible by the road leading to the village of Assevillers (carried on July 3) on the one hand, and with the Somme valley by the road which ends at the bridges and highway of Feuillères (also captured on July 3).

The brick and rubble houses of Herbécourt stood at this cross-roads.

ON LEAVING HERBÉCOURT—GERMAN BLOCKHOUSE AT THE CORNER OF THE ROADS TO CAPPY (*on the right*) AND DOMPIERRE (*on the left*).

GERMAN TRENCHES ON THE HERBÉCOURT PLATEAU.

FEUILLÈRES CHURCH AND VILLAGE (*not in Itinerary*).
*On the canal between Frise and Biaches, they were violently
bombarded in 1916.*

Nothing remains of them now, except a few walls, beams and fragments of the timber frameworks of the battered farm-houses.

The façade, steeple and roofing of the church were destroyed. Only a few battered fragments of the sides, walls, and choir are still standing.

Leave Herbécourt by the G.C. 71. A blockhouse for machine-guns is seen on the left, near the last ruins.

The road runs across a bare plateau, then passes through the destroyed hamlet of **Becquincourt,** *after which* **Dompierre** *is reached.*

Dompierre was the central point in the zone of attack on July 1, 1916. It was carried on the first day, after a brilliant assault, together with the neighbouring hamlet of Becquincourt and Bussus farm, to the south. The German system of defence-works comprised three successive lines of trenches connected with one another by communication trenches, and reinforced with redoubts and concrete shelters for machine-guns. Here were to be found the " Gatz " trench, and the " Misery " and " Thirst " communication-trenches. The bombardment which preceded the attack was terrific, the whole area

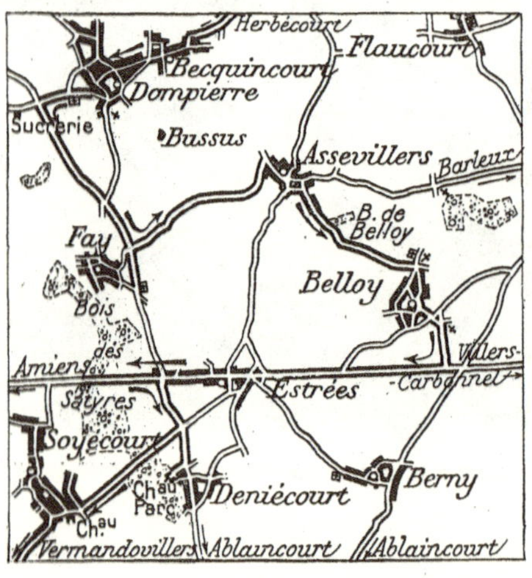

being upturned by the shells ; not a single square yard of the ground was left intact.

The village was not spared by the bombardments ; most of the houses were reduced to shapeless heaps of bricks and broken beams. The site of the church is marked by a heap of white stones, higher than the others.

After passing through Dompierre, take the road to Fay, on the left.

The ruined **sugar-refinery** of Dompierre *is on the right,* 200 *yards farther on (photos, p.* 121).

The Dompierre Sugar Refinery was within the French first lines, but the village itself, although close by, was still in enemy hands. The Germans attacked the refinery for two years, without being able to capture it. It was, however, cut to pieces by the shells. The brick walls crumbled away, but the steel framework resisted. Numbers of twisted and rusty pipes, iron plates, cocks and vats, all disjointed, broken, and out of shape, are still to be seen.

Quite close to, at a crossroad, stands a calvary which is now famous. The ground all around was churned up by the shells ; only one hit the calvary,

DOMPIERRE.   THE SUGAR REFINERY IN 1916.

carrying away an arm of Christ.   The cross remained intact, and supported the mutilated statue to the last.

Pass through **Fay,** *2 km. 500 farther on.*

In the neighbouring sector of Dompierre, mine explosions succeeded one another almost incessantly at Fay, during the trench warfare period, especially in 1915–1916 ; the official communiqués often mentioned this fighting as being extremely violent.

The French and German trenches ran along the western outskirts of the village and were protected by very powerful defence-works, difficult to approach in the open.   Recourse was, therefore, to mines.

The Somme offensive put an end to these sanguinary engagements, which had brought about no great change in the French or German positions. Fay, completely razed, was carried on July 1.

Among the ruins, the road turns at right-angles to the left (leave the Estrées road to the right).   3 km. beyond Fay, **Assevillers,** *built on a hill and entirely destroyed, is reached.*

DOMPIERRE.   THE SUGAR REFINERY IN 1919.
On the left : Road to Faucancourt ; On the right : Road to Chuignes.

Pass through Assevillers, turning to the right, on entering.   On leaving, take the road to **Belloy-en-Santerre**, *on the right.*

Before reaching Belloy, the road descends into a hollow (see defence-works and shelters), and skirts **Belloy Wood**, the trees of which were cut to pieces by shell-fire.   The wood lies on an eminence, from the top of which are seen the ruins of a castle.   Fine view towards Biaches.

Capture of Belloy-en-Santerre

Debouching from Assevillers (carried on July 3, 1916) and progressing north of Estrées, a number of French units reached the outskirts of Belloy-en-Santerre on July 4 ;   this village was powerfully fortified and formed an important strong-point in the German second line defences.

That famous regiment, the Foreign Legion, whose flag is decorated with

FAY VILLAGE, AS THE WAR LEFT IT, SEEN FROM THE ASSEVILLERS ROAD (*Itinerary*).
On the left : Road to Estreés ; In front : Road from Dompierre.

the *Legion d'Honneur,* and whose innumerable exploits have won for it many mentions in the Orders of the Army, was ordered on July 4, at 6 p.m., to carry the position immediately at the point of the bayonet.

Deployed in battle formation, they charged across a flat meadow 900 yards broad.   When 300 yards from their objective, machine-guns hidden in the path from Estrées to Belloy were suddenly unmasked, and a deadly fire mowed down the French ranks.   The 9th and 11th Companies sustained particularly heavy losses, all the officers falling.   One of these companies reached the

BELLOY-EN-SANTERRE, SEEN FROM THE SITE OF THE CHURCH.
In the middle: Road from Assevillers; At the back: Belloy Wood.

objective under the command of the mess corporal. Belloy was captured and 750 Germans were taken prisoners.

The enemy immediately launched counter-attack upon counter-attack. Terrible fighting went on throughout the night. In the early morning, the Germans regained a footing in Belloy, and entered the park of the Castle, where three sections of the Legion were surrounded.

A second-lieutenant received orders to restore the situation with the remnants of a company. Posting his men along the Belloy-Barleux road (G.C. 79), he cut the line of retreat of the Germans, who had entered the park. The latter endeavoured to break through, with a detachment of disarmed prisoners in their midst.

The lieutenant shouted to the prisoners to lie down, then ordered his men to fire on the standing Germans. The latter surrendered, with the exception of a handful who attempted to carry away a wounded French officer. The newly-released prisoners, although unarmed, dashed to the rescue of the commander and brought him back in triumph.

Belloy was almost entirely reconquered, and when in the evening a new counter-attack was launched, their assaulting waves were literally mowed down.

The terrific bombardments which took place before and after the capture of Belloy-en-Santerre entirely annihilated the village.

The road at Belloy passes by a large French cemetery and, a little further on, the ruins of the church. *Take a newly-made road leading to the Amiens-St. Quentin road. Turn to the right, towards Estrées (3 km.) and pass (on the right), a British then a large French cemetery.* **Estrées** *is next reached.*

MILITARY CEMETERY TO THE EAST OF ESTRÉES.

Estrées

This village was built along the wide road (an old Roman causeway) which runs from Amiens to Vermand, and thence to Saint-Quentin (G.C. 201). This absolutely straight road formed the separation line between the Chaulnes sector and the Somme battlefield properly so-called, where the Franco-British attack began on July 1, 1916, and which extended along both banks of the Somme, as far as the small river Ancre.

Estrées was one of the points where the fighting, begun on July 1, was most violent.

The French, whose first-lines at the time ran east of Foucourt, carried the advance trenches which covered Estrées, along the Amiens—St.-Quentin road, after most desperate fighting, and finally gained a footing in the village.

The photograph opposite shows the condition of the road after its capture by the French ; the causeway had disappeared and, on the shell-torn ground there were hardly any traces left of the German trenches which had everywhere fallen in.

Estrées village had to be captured house by house. On the evening of July 4, after three days' fighting, the Germans held only the eastern part of the village. For the next twenty days, about 200 of them hung on desperately to it, holding back the assailants with machine-guns posted in the cellars, which fired through the narrow vent-holes. To overcome this resistance, which prevented all advance north or south, it was necessary to sacrifice these houses, and for six consecutive hours 9-in., 11-in., and 15-in. shells

ESTRÉES.   SITE OF THE CEMETERY IN AUGUST, 1916.

THE AMIENS ST. QUENTIN ROAD IN SATYRES WOOD,
WEST OF ESTRÉES (1916).

pounded this small area. Only fifteen survivors were found in the ruined foundations; the rest of the German garrison had been wiped out.

This terrible struggle utterly destroyed the village. Its site and the surrounding land form a chaotic waste; all traces of the former landmarks have disappeared.

Keep along G.C. 201, towards Amiens. The remains of **Satyres Wood** are in a hollow of the road, about 1 km. beyond Estrées.

Satyres Wood

The remains of this once fine wood extend from this point of the road to the village of Fay, 1,500 yards to the right. From 1914 to 1916 it formed part of the German first-line defence-works, and was covered with entrenchments of all kinds.

On July 1, 1916, the French carried the whole wood, promptly re-organised the defence-works, and used them against their former occupants.

A CORNER OF SATYRES WOOD.

SATYRES WOOD.
*The German Post of Commandment seen in the photograph below,
is under this road.*

Numerous cottages and shelters hidden by the trees were used as billets by the enemy troops in this sector. The officers occupied a special quarter. A large signboard with the inscription, " Durchgang nur für Offiziere," interdicted its access to the common soldiers. All the shelters were spacious and comfortably furnished with beds, tables, armchairs, hangings, chandeliers, and even pianos—all taken from the neighbouring villages. Some of the cottages were decorated outside, and sometimes bore inscriptions like the following, carved on the door of a post of commandment :—

" Macht Joffre auch ein böses Gesicht
Hier treffen uns seine Granaten nicht."

(Joffre may roll his eyes : his shells cannot reach us here.)

The French soldiers called this wood "Satyres Wood," as they found women's clothing in various places.

SATYRES WOOD. GERMAN POST OF COMMANDMENT
UNDER THE ROAD (*see above*).

DENIÉCOURT WOOD AT SUNSET.

Return to the entrance to Estrées, and take the road on the right to **Deniécourt.**
On entering the village, take on foot the small road on the right to **the ruins of**
Deniécourt Château, situated in a devastated park.

Deniécourt village lies about 2 km. (by road) east of **Soyécourt.** Across
the fields, the distance is shorter, and it was covered in a single rush on the
day Soyécourt was captured, after which the advance was stayed. The
second German line ran through Deniécourt, which was fortified accordingly.
The most important defence-works were those around the château, which
latter formed the key of the whole position. Deep shelters had been made
under the château itself and also in the surrounding park. The whole formed
an inextricable maze of trenches, fortified works, machine-gun posts, traps
and barbed-wire entanglements, which had to be reduced by shell-fire. The
castle was razed to the ground, the defences in the park destroyed and the
ground levelled.

On the day of attack, the fighting was none the less desperate in the
neighbourhood, and afterwards inside the village. The French advance was
several times held by furious counter-attacks, and it was only on September 18
that the whole position could be surrounded and carried, after several days of
bitter fighting. Of Deniécourt village, château and park, not a stone or a
tree remained.

Return to the car and take the road already followed (G.C. 164) back to the
fork (300 yards north of the village), then the road to **Soyécourt** *(G.C. 79),*

SOYÉCOURT CHURCH IN 1916.

on the left. At the entrance to Soyécourt the ruins of a château—of which only the base of one tower remains—will be seen on the left.

For nearly two years the French first lines ran close to the western outskirts of this village, which lies at the bottom of a ravine. On several occasions the communiqués mentioned sharp fighting around here, which was, however, merely of local importance.

It was only on September 4, 1916, that decisive fighting took place here, when the French, after a long and terrific bombardment, carried the village in a single rush, and progressed beyond it in the direction of Deniécourt.

Leaving Soyécourt, keep along G.C. 79 to **Vermandovillers** *(2 km.).*

On September 4, 1916, the village was attacked from the east and north. Progress was slow, and marked by fierce fighting from house to house. Vermandovillers was only captured in its entirety on September 17.

At the fork in the village, take the left-hand road (G.C. 143) to **Chaulnes.**

VERMANDOVILLERS.

Chaulnes

Chaulnes Wood is crossed 1 km. this side of Chaulnes.   Violent attacks were delivered by the French in the vicinity of this wood.   The large number of soldiers' graves along both sides of the road form an impressive sight.

Several hundred yards beyond the fork formed in the road by the junction with

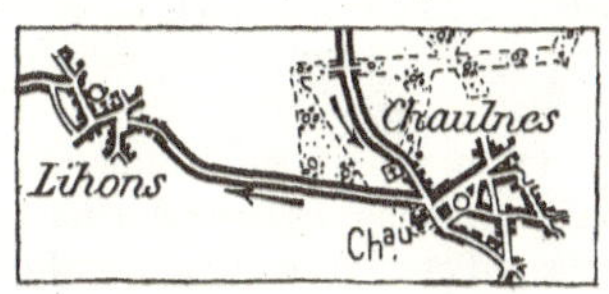

G.C. 206 coming from Lihons, turn to the left, and enter **Chaulnes** in front of the ruins of the large eighteenth century church.   A few

gments of crumbling walls are all that remain (*photos, p.* 130).

Chaulnes, the chief town of one of the "cantons" in the "Département" of the Somme, was situated at the junction of several railroads.   In 1914, the Germans turned the place into a fortress, and made it the chief strong-point of their system of defence-works south of the Somme.   Traces of the powerful fortifications—the first lines of which were only carried in 1916—may still be seen along and near G.C. 206, amidst the churned-up ground.

The village was flanked on the north and north-west by dense woods, which were entirely destroyed by the bombardments. These woods were full of fortified works, trenches and posts for machine-guns, protected by wire entanglements.

On September 4, 1916, the French reached the outskirts of these woods, but failed in their attempts to carry them entirely. The Germans maintained themselves there till March, 1917, on positions sufficiently strong to allow them to hold Chaulnes, this village being outflanked everywhere else.

Chaulnes was occupied only when the Germans fell back upon the Hindenburg Line. The British having relieved the French troops during the winter of 1916, from the Somme to the Avre, entered the place almost without striking a blow on March 18, 1917.

The Germans recaptured Chaulnes in March, 1918. On August 8 of the same year—their front having been pierced before Amiens—they were forced

CHAULNES, GENERAL VIEW OF THE TOWN.

CHAULNES. THE CHÂTEAU.

to evacuate the Montdidier " pocket " and to retreat to the outskirts of Chaulnes. They reoccupied their positions of the trench warfare period, and the remains of their ancient defence-works were still strong enough to enable them to hold up the British pursuit. The town was only carried on August 28, after being surrounded.

Chaulnes was razed to the ground. The low brick-and-rubble houses which lined the wide straight streets sheltered a population of about 1,250 inhabitants. Very few of them escaped total destruction.

Return along the same road by which Chaulnes was entered and follow it to the junction of G.C. 143 with G.C. 206, at the exit of the town. The ruins of the **château** are seen on the left, near the fork.

This sumptuous château was built in the seventeenth century by the de Luynes family, for whose benefit Chaulnes was raised to the rank of a duchy-peerage in 1621. Madame de Sévigné stayed there in 1689, and extolled its magnificence and grandeur. It was surrounded by a vast park, which she compared to that of Versailles.

CHAULNES. THE CHÂTEAU PARK.
In the foreground : Fragment of the entrance gate between the graves of two German officers.

The outbuildings were still standing when the late war broke out ; to-day they form a shapeless accumulation of *débris*. The park was entirely cut up with German entrenchments, of which only a few concrete machine-gun posts and underground shelters with concrete entrances remain. The fine old trees of the park were reduced by the shells to mutilated stumps.

Near the entrance-gate of the château is a powerful system of defence-works, consisting of a machine-gun blockhouse and inter-communicating underground shelters, the entrances to which may be seen near the side of the road.

After visiting the château, keep along G.C. 206, towards Lihons.

Skirt the southern end of Chaulnes Wood, near which, on either side of the road, are two powerful concrete blockhouses and other German defence-works.

ENTRANCE TO GERMAN SHELTER AND BLOCKHOUSE IN THE CHÂTEAU PARK.

Lihons (3 *km. beyond Chaulnes*) *is next reached.*

Lying at an important junction of several roads, Lihons was already in enemy hands when the front-line trenches were made.

Starting from Rosières-en-Santerre at the end of October, 1914, the French first reached and carried Lihons after a series of fierce engagements, then progressed beyond it, in the direction of Chaulnes (only 3 km. distant). For more than a month the Germans counter-attacked almost daily, in an endeavour to reconquer the lost trenches, but were each time repulsed.

Exasperated by their failure, they then bombarded the town without respite, and when the Allied Offensive of 1916 began this shelling was further intensified.

Lihons, a small country town, the streets of which—bordered with low houses—ran in all directions from a large, central square, was quickly reduced to ruins. The houses fell down one after the other, and the church suffered irreparable damage.

The church was one of considerable interest. The choir, transept and lower part of the tower, built at the intersection of the transept, were finely proportioned and dated from the thirteenth century. The other parts of the building were fifteenth century.

In July, 1916, the church had already lost its tower, roof and vaulting, but the outside walls, the pillars separating the three naves and the three gables of the main façade were still standing. Three months later nothing was left but fragments of broken walls, amidst a shapeless accumulation of *débris* (*photos, p.* 133).

LIHONS CHURCH BEFORE THE WAR.

LIHONS CHURCH IN 1916.

LIHONS CHURCH IN 1919.
On the left: The road to Vermandovillers.

Further fighting took place in the ruins of Lihons in 1918. On August 8, British troops, starting from the region of Villers-Bretonneux—Hangard, reached Lihons on the 10th. Preceded by light tanks, armoured cars and cavalry patrols, the Australians immediately entered the village, drove out the enemy and captured a complete Divisional staff. It was in vain that the Germans launched numerous counter-attacks in an endeavour to recapture the village and clear the approaches to Chaulnes, where they attempted to establish their lines of resistance. They could only delay the British advance for a few days.

At Lihons, leave the Vermandovillers road (G.C. 79) on the right and take that on the left. Turn to the right, in the village, leave the church on the right, and take the Vauvillers road (G.C. 206) on the left.

At the fork, about 500 yards beyond Lihons, leave the left-hand road to Rosières, and take that on the right (still G.C. 206). This road skirts a small wood, on the right, in which are many graves and gun-emplacements. *The village of* **Rosières-en-Santerre** *comes into view, on the left.*

At the crossing of several roads, 3 km. beyond Lihons, take the newly-made road on the right to Herleville. The large French "Camp des Chasseurs" cemetery (*photo below*) *is on the left, about 1 km. this side of the village of* **Herleville** (completely devastated), *which is next reached.*

At the entrance to the village, a "calvary" is passed, of which nothing remains but the stumps of four large trees. Keep straight on through the ruined village to the G.C. 201 (main road from Amiens to Péronne), *1 km. beyond it. Turn to the left and return direct to Amiens via* **Lamotte-en-Santerre** *and* **Villers-Bretonneux,** both of which villages were badly damaged during the fighting of 1918.

A short distance before Longueau, G.C. 201 joins N. 35, which take to the right. Amiens is entered by the Chaussée Périgord.

ALPHABETICAL LIST OF THE PLACES MENTIONED IN THIS WORK.

The figures in heavy type indicate the pages on which there are illustrations.

CONTENTS

A VISIT TO THE BATTLEFIELDS.

www.ingramcontent.com/pod-product-compliance
Lightning Source LLC
Chambersburg PA
CBHW031259060726
47590CB00003B/975